UNTAMABLE

©2021 by Nahla Khaddage Bou-Diab

UNTAMABLE Copyright © 2021 by Dr. Nahla Khaddage Bou-Diab, Oneness Offshore. All rights reserved. No part of this publication may be reproduced, distributed, or transmitted in any form or by any means, including photocopying, recording, or other electronic or mechanical methods, without the prior written permission of the publisher, except in the case of brief quotations embodied in reviews and certain other noncommercial uses permitted by copyright law.

For information contact Dr. Nahla Khaddage Bou-Diab, Oneness Offshore at www.NahlaBouDiab.com.

Published by ONENESS OFFSHORE SAL. ONENESS OFFSHORE SAL, its logos, and marks are the trademarks of ONENESS OFFSHORE. All other brand names and product names used in this book are trade names, service marks, trademarks, or registered trademarks of their respective owners. The publisher and the book are not associated with any product or vendor mentioned in this book. None of the companies referenced within the book have endorsed the book. The material in this book is intended for educational purposes. It is not meant to take the place of diagnosis, and treatment by a qualified medical practitioner or therapist. No expressed or implied guarantee of the effects of the use of the recommendations can be given or liability taken.

ONENESS OFFSHORE

The Library of Congress Cataloging-in-Publication Data

Names: Khaddage Bou-Diab, Nahla, author.
Title: Untamable: Claim Your Power, Live Fearlessly, and Become Unstoppable / Dr. Nahla Khaddage Bou-Diab.
Other Titles: Untamable
Description: Oneness Offshore, 2021.
Identifiers: **LCCN**
Subjects: LCSH: Memoir, Self-actualization, Personal Growth, Empowerment
BISAC: SELF-HELP / Memoir / Personal Growth / Happiness / Empowerment
LC record available at https://lccn.loc.gov

Copyright Registration Number: TXu002245280

ISBN: 978-1-647044-58-9

First edition: May 2021

UNTAMABLE

Claim Your Power, Live Fearlessly,
and Become Unstoppable.

DR. NAHLA KHADDAGE BOU-DIAB

Praise for *Untamable*

"Part novel, part self-help guide, *Untamable* is a compelling personal story of one woman's ability to turn challenges into opportunities, and the lessons we can all take from her journey. In the first half, Dr. Nahla Khaddage Bou-Diab shares the personal and professional struggles she faced throughout her life, from assimilating to new countries, to navigating low family expectations for girls, to managing workplace harassment. She then uses these experiences to illustrate how we can all shift our thinking, and - in her words - "to see challenges as opportunities for growth." How? By adopting core guiding principles that help us achieve greater happiness and reach our full potential. I can't think of a more important message."

- Catherine Sanderson, PhD, Author of *"The Positive Shift"*

"An inspiring story of how letting go and being one with the universe can let come exactly the life that is ours to lead and learn from."

- Ginny Whitelaw, PhD, author of *"Resonate"*, CEO of Institute for Zen Leadership

"Every person has a purpose, a calling, and unique dreams that are ours alone. Dr. Nahla Khaddage Bou-Diab's insightful book demonstrates how to thrive, meet life's challenges head-on with confidence, providing a pathway to understanding how to manifest our dreams and live an authentic life."
- Maryann Ridini Spencer, award-winning screenwriter/producer, Simply Delicious Living TV host and author of the Kate Grace Novels *"Lady in the Window," "The Paradise Table,"* and *"Secrets of Grace Manor"*

"*Untamable* gives you the straight path to light up your heart and connect with the love in you and the universe. Dr. Khaddage Bou-Diab, through her transparency, shares her pain and light, dualities and integrity, and the essence of what makes each human being a success story - Love"
- Dr. Foojan Zeine - Renown Psychotherapist and the author of *"Life Reset: The Awareness Integration Path to Create the Life You Want"*

"In *Untamable: Claim Your Power, Live Fearlessly, and Become Unstoppable*, Nahla Bou-Diab deep dives fearlessly into her own journey with courage and optimism. Her insights offer a powerful light to any reader stumbling through the darkness of life's adversities. If you are looking for a way to find the blessings in misfortune, let Dr. Bou-Diab be your guide."
- Laurie Nadel, Ph.D. *"The Five Gifts: Discovering Hope, Healing and Strength When Disaster Strikes"*

"Everyday empowerment is at the heart of my work as a Sophrologist. This book beautifully illustrates how you can tap into the power of your dreams and hopes to positively transform your circumstances."

- Dominique Antiglio, Sophrologist, Author of *"The Life-Changing Power of Sophrology"* and BeSophro Founder

This book is dedicated to:

My father, because his fears ignited a volcano of
emotions in me,
My mother, because her sacrifices fueled the
volcano with strengths,
My husband, because his love calmed the volcano,
My sons, because loving them motivated me
to turn the volcano into a piece of art that I am
sharing with the world.

Contents

Introduction	**XIII**
How This Book Can Help You	XIV
Why I Wrote This book	XV
Your Evolution Begins Now	XVIII

Part I - MY STORY   1

Chapter 1 - Growing Up in Lebanon and Canada   3

This Place	4
Dreaming of Horses	8
One Piece of Feta Cheese	10
My Best Friend	14
Death Was All Around	17
Girls Don't Need to Attend University	23

Chapter 2 - My Career   29

The Branch Manager	30
Going to Night School	34
The Perfect Life	36
Darkness in Toronto	39
The Scent of Flowers	41
My Dream Guy	45
Total Inner Peace	50
Is This Who I Am?	53
I Was Nothing	55
An Urge to Leave	60

Chapter 3 - Back in Lebanon   63

Success at Work	63
Spiritual Nourishment	65

Chapter 4 - A Journey to Wake Up   69

Hello, Universe	69
Signs from the Universe	72

Part II - MY LESSONS   81

Chapter 5 - Where I Am Today   83
What I've Learned from Life   86

Chapter 6 - Where Are You Today?   91
Is It About Happiness?   95
You Don't Need to Suffer Anymore   98

Chapter 7 - The Powers Around Us   101
The Power of Society   102
The Power of Learning   111
The Power of Fear   117
Our Inner Powers   121
We Are in Control   127

Chapter 8 - One Core Step: Connect, Trust, Accept   141
How to Connect   143
How to Trust   145
How to Accept   147

Chapter 9 - The Five Guiding Principles   149
Feel Gratitude   150
Observe   152
Nourish Your Whole Self   156
Dream   158
Release Your Expectations   162

Chapter 10 - My Parting Gift to You   165

Resources   167

Introduction

We all have an innate ability to dream, to envision the things we need and want in order to feel happy and whole. We are able to imagine our future selves thriving in a specific place, with loved ones. We can visualize achieving our goals. Humans have this unique, universal ability, which is so powerful that it can save lives. I know this to be true, because scientific evidence supports it, and because dreaming saved my life.

It's hard to dream when your dreams are crushed, though. Maybe your parents forced you to abide by strict or stringent rules, which made you rebel. Maybe your employer or boss routinely shuts down your ideas. Perhaps your environment is dangerous and you feel helpless. Or maybe you've been the victim of a crime. Perhaps the tenets of your religion or the social norms of your culture feel crushing, limiting, or oppressive. It's possible that you are in a relationship with a partner who makes you feel unworthy. Maybe you are simply feeling stuck and hopeless.

If any of these scenarios describe you—if you have ever been made to feel afraid, angry, bullied, belittled, or unsafe—please take thirty seconds right now to pause, close your eyes, and allow yourself to dream of whatever being safe, empowered, and happy means to you. Just thirty seconds. Right now.

I invite you to take this time for yourself, not as a gimmick but rather as a reminder that you have this gift already inside you. You already know exactly what you need—you have inherent wisdom, potential, and power. It's time for you to access and activate this gift. This book will show you how.

How This Book Can Help You

This book is written for my fellow humans who have felt (or are still feeling) victimized by big or small life challenges; there is absolutely hope for you. You can overcome your hardships. This book will teach you how to do that.

You will learn *one core step* and *five simple principles* for achieving your dreams, even in the face of difficulties. The teachings in this book are informed by science-backed data, and the exercises are grounded in evidence-based therapeutic practices - including mindfulness, compassion, and gratitude - as well as acceptance and commitment therapy. *Untamable* will teach you how to:

- Find and express your voice
- Free yourself from restraining negative thoughts
- Notice and effectively respond to fear
- Let go of what you cannot control
- Build the security and confidence necessary to pursue suppressed dreams
- Gain present-moment awareness
- Start a gratitude practice

- Use visualization to plan for and experience goal achievement
- Connect to and trust in a higher power
- Activate your inherent potential and wisdom
- Practice whole-body self-care for body, mind, and spirit

Evolving your thinking and transforming your life from one of suffering to one of achievement is neither easy nor quick, but it is possible! You will need to commit to trying something new and different, possibly even scary, which may also go against what peers, managers, community leaders, or even loved ones endorse. But keep in mind that this book is for *you,* not them. You will be looking at *your* values and aspirations, not theirs. This is *your* life, not theirs. Make it the life you dream of.

Why I Wrote This book

I was excited as I walked into the conference room to attend my first company meeting after being recruited as a senior consultant. I was thrilled to connect with new colleagues, share my ideas, hear inspirational strategies, and feel a sense of belonging as our diverse voices shaped a collective vision.

As I took my seat, I noticed a number of Koosh™ balls in the center of the conference table.

"What are those for?" I asked the person next to me, pointing to the tennis-ball-sized brightly colored orbs made of soft rubber strands. I was curious to know what role they might play in an innovative team-building exercise.

"Oh! Those Koosh™ balls are a fun way to keep everyone on task. You see, if anyone drifts from the subject, shares thoughts not directly connected to the objective at hand, or has too outlandish of an idea, you can grab a ball and chuck it at the person. It keeps everyone focused and on task."

I was horrified.

"Don't worry," my colleague said, responding to the disconcerted expression on my face. "They don't hurt." And with that, she playfully tossed one into my lap.

In that moment, recollections of all the oppression I had fought against to have a seat at this table came rushing to my awareness. Practically my whole life had been a fight to free myself from other people's control, fears, and rules. During my entire childhood, I lived in fear of doing the "wrong" thing. At eight years old, I couldn't play with other children for fear of soiling my clothes and upsetting my mother. At twelve years old, I was ridiculed by teachers and bullied by peers for not speaking or looking like them. At sixteen, because of war, I was told where to live, what to do, and what to think. When I was seventeen, I was denied a higher education, because "a girl doesn't need to go to university." And that same year, I was threatened with being fired if I didn't submit to my manager's advances. It was as if everyone had an opinion of what I needed to do and how I needed to live—everyone but me!

I was not dreaming of material objects. I was dreaming of basic life necessities: to be safe, to have individual freedom, to have enough to eat, to be strong, to be kind, and to be loved unconditionally. I was hungry to dream, and dreaming made me happy.

Sitting in that conference room, yet another person, this time my employer, was determined to limit dreaming—because efficiency dictates focused thoughts, and dreaming is a waste of time.

But is this how life is supposed to be? Driven by rules that others impose? Is this how we unleash passion? Is suppressing dreams a good strategy for success? Can we foster creativity by putting a limit on ideas? What is human potential? And how can it ever be realized if we're controlling how people think and crushing their ideas with a wallop of a Koosh™ ball?

In part I of this book, I share my personal story: growing up in Lebanon and Canada, experiencing two wars firsthand, struggling to assimilate as an immigrant in a foreign country, tiptoeing around the stringent rules of my parents' culture, navigating workplace inequities, fighting for an education, achieving career success, finding love, and overcoming a health crisis.

Yes, I've had a challenging life, but my story is not a sad one. It is a beautiful story about human potential, about the inherent inner strength of all people, about the power of our thoughts, and about the importance of establishing a strong connection with the universe. The purpose of writing about my life—both in hardships and in triumphs—is to show you how difficulties can drive our evolution.

My calling is to convince you that life is not about what you go through; it's about what you do with your experiences.

I offer you my story as a personal invitation to shift your thinking, to see challenges as opportunities for growth. I hope my story helps you discover your own power and how to use your natural abilities to connect with our universal power. That is why, in part II of this book, I facilitate this process by sharing with you a core step and five guiding principles that I used to reach my own potential and that I hope will add tremendous value to your journey toward unleashing your own potential.

Your Evolution Begins Now

Let's shift your life from being one of victimization to one of empowerment. Your reality is your own creation. Events—no matter how painful—can be a major force in discovering all that you are truly capable of. And as your thinking evolves and circumstances improve, you'll see that my story is no longer guiding you, but rather that there is a universal force guiding you and sending you messages. All you need to do is be in receiving mode. I'll show you what has worked for me and countless others.

Finally, I hope this book will inspire you to calm your mind. Because only when you have a calm mind will you be ready to enjoy your journey and start asking questions. Only then can you see beyond the clutter and take in the messages offered to you. Only then can you be truly open to learning, evolving your spirituality, and achieving your personal dreams.

I invite you now to listen to my story. And as you read, I invite you to reflect on your own story. Moreover, I invite you to begin to change the narrative of your story. Start a new chapter of your life. An entire universe awaits you.

Part I

MY STORY

Chapter 1

Growing Up in Lebanon and Canada

I was born into a middle-class family, in a third-world country, to parents who loved me and my siblings with an unbending intensity. Yes, I was loved, but I didn't always feel this way. In fact, most of the time it seemed as if my parents cared more about what other people thought of them and their actions than they cared about me. Their rigid compliance with social norms seemed to take precedence over everything—even our own happiness at times.

My father was a "good man" who, in his drive to be respected by society, suppressed his love and applied discipline to ensure that we—his family—never put his reputation at risk. My dad conformed to society so well that all I saw was a conservative, traditional man who imposed tremendous pressure on his family so that his community would be pleased with him.

When I was a small child, my father would hug me, hold me, and show affection. I cherished our time together. Every day, I would wait for him to arrive home from work, then hide, and the moment he walked into the house, I would run and hug his leg, surprising him. I was so small, my head barely reached his knees. He would pick me up and laugh, making me feel a sense of accomplishment that my surprise attack had worked yet again.

Like my dad, my mother was totally committed to her family and ensured that the family's reputation always came first, even if meeting this expectation was exhausting to her. She was a perfect homemaker. She gave us the best of everything: the best food, the best clothes, and the best manners. She invested her time in helping us with our homework and making sure we were raised perfectly.

As a teenager, my mom had had dreams of becoming an artist and a fashion designer. But these dreams were quickly squashed by the accepted social norms back then. She needed to play the role that society designed for her as a woman: to value marriage, have children, and excel at being a homemaker. Her ambitions were irrelevant; she needed to focus on getting married and forming a good family, and that is exactly what she did to become a "good woman."

This Place

Ever since I was a small child, even before I turned five, I felt that I didn't belong in "this place." Although I couldn't describe my feelings until later, I had always sensed a huge gap between what I wanted my life to be and the life that was possible for me. In my young mind, life was about living, feeling, sensing, discovering, and learning. But the environment in which I was living, life seemed to be about suppression, getting by with the least damage possible, and clambering to stay safe.

As I got a little older, I felt like I was in jail—even though I had never actually been in one! And, at times, I felt as if my life was worse than jail. My young mind reasoned that at least a real jail is recognized as such and carries a release date, a date when you will be freed. But "this place" had a permanent sentence, with no specific release date and no option for parole.

I realized very early on that my life sentence could be made worse by not abiding by all the rules. In other words, I had to grow up *obediently*. If I were obedient, I could ensure a "good" reputation, so that eventually a "good man" would marry me. A "good girl" does what she is told, does not question, nor does she want anything beyond what she is allowed to have. As a girl, my actions were governed by understanding the rules and never breaking them, even if the rules deprived me of my dreams and ambitions. Breaking a rule was so risky that I was constantly worried about doing something wrong.

When I was three years old, I was sent to a private Christian school known for its extreme disciplinary measures and the high quality of education it offered. Going to this strict school driven by rules and punishment positioned me as a privileged child and added to the expectation of how perfect I needed to be. Students would regularly get hit for speaking out of turn, be humiliated by teachers in front of the entire class if they broke the rules, or get screamed at for not doing well in the assigned readings.

One day, I watched in fear as a teacher humiliated one of my classmates for wearing socks that were not white. Wearing socks of any other color was a horrific breach of the school policy, and the humiliation was just as horrific! I never wanted to go through such an experience, so I made sure I never broke the rules. I followed the dress code perfectly. I never made mistakes—at least I tried not to make mistakes.

Another day, a couple of years later, while I was sitting at my desk doing an assignment, my teacher summoned me to her desk. I was shaking with worry because I knew she had been grading our homework while we were doing classwork. She looked at me with disappointment and said, "For a straight-A student, you really messed up." Then, in front of all my classmates, she pinched my ear so hard that it started bleeding. Later it got infected. I promised myself never to go through that humiliation again. From then on, and until we immigrated to Canada, my average was A+. All my effort was focused on protecting myself from humiliation.

I was such a pretty and elegant girl that people would praise my mother for my perfect clothes and my clean appearance. They would commend her for doing a great job, while scoffing at the kids with mud-streaked clothes who were, apparently, not raised properly. Once, when I was six years old, I stood primly watching my friends playing in the garden, climbing trees, touching earth. Sand filled their pockets, their hands were muddy. I wanted to touch the mud so badly, but I was so worried about dirtying my pretty yellow silk skirt—yes, silk!— I knew I couldn't play with the other children. Playing was not allowed if it would damage my reputation.

Mud was not in my future, but I knew a husband was. Although I don't recall my parents saying that my purpose in life was to marry a "good man"—at least not until I was older—it was implied by the social setting in which I lived. So, at six years old, I allowed myself to dream of the perfect husband. And this perfect husband happened to be Ghassan, the son of my parents' best friends. Ghassan and I had barely exchanged a handful of words at this point, considering he was a teenager and I a child, but I fantasized about him nevertheless. This dream was so important to my happiness, and so vivid, that I shared it with my mother. It was one of the few times I ever spoke without being prompted.

No, I wasn't shy. I didn't even consider myself to have a quiet disposition. It's that I was so terrified of saying the "wrong" thing and getting into trouble that I just stayed silent. Because I didn't always understand the rules as a child, it felt safer to strive to be perfect: work hard, get good grades, don't get dirty, don't do anything wrong, don't say anything bad… The effort it took to keep a tally of all the things I was not allowed to do was exhausting.

But despite my worries and my anxiety, I had this powerful belief that I was not alone—that God would guide me and protect me. I figured that the only explanation for this level of cruelty was that I was being tested. I felt that if I was "good" and tolerated my surroundings, I would be rewarded for my behavior. My belief that God was watching me and that he would make everything all right triggered my acceptance of things. This acceptance of his protective force allowed me to focus on getting through whatever situation I was in. I reasoned that any difficulty I was facing was not permanent—even if it felt that way at times—and so I learned to be tolerant, to go through the storm quietly and patiently, waiting for it to end.

This belief in God also allowed me to dream—not just of my future husband but of other things I wanted. One important dream at the time was to grow up safely, without humiliation or abuse at school. I figured that once I grew up, I would be free. So my goal was to do well in school and graduate.

Dreaming of Horses

When I turned eight, war erupted in my country, and my father decided to immigrate to Canada, where we had family. The plan was to live with our relative there until we got set up on our own. Every night until we left Lebanon, I pictured what I knew of Canada from Western movies, and I started dreaming of life there. My three siblings and I would live on a big farm, we would have horses. I would be able to run in nature, walk barefoot and feel the earth. I pictured myself free, riding a horse, feeling the wind on my face, and running with no limits. No one would scrutinize me or judge me. I would be living with no rules and therefore no possibility of breaking any rules. I would be free of "this place" and the jail I was in.

I didn't feel sad about leaving. I packed a small bag containing souvenirs from my closest friends. I didn't care to take anything else with me.

Our journey to Canada was difficult. Because the airport was closed, we had to travel on a commercial boat to Cyprus. Being on a commercial boat meant no drinking water and no cabins, and people slept on the deck. But my father paid the boat's captain to rent his room. We were fortunate to have this small luxury, but I don't remember it well. All I remember from this two-day voyage was the overwhelming thirst I felt.

When we arrived in Cyprus, we lifted our tired spirits by talking about our shared dream: the color of each of the horses, the names we'd give them, what time we would wake up to feed them, and how wonderful it was going to be to ride them.

We traveled on a passenger boat, then took a ten-hour car ride to Jordan for our scheduled flight to Canada. After this long and uncomfortable journey, we arrived in Canada in 1976.

None of us could speak or read English. We didn't know our way around. And my father's relative made it very clear that he didn't want to feel our presence in his home. So we had to make sure we didn't eat too much of his food or make a lot of noise. With four kids between the ages of five and twelve, these requirements were challenging.

My father got a job as a security guard. He left the house at 11:00 p.m. and came back at 7:00 a.m. There were times when he would get lost because he didn't know his way around. Since he didn't speak English, he couldn't ask anyone for help. Other times, he would be so exhausted that he would fall asleep on the bus and miss his stop. Some nights, he would be so stressed and anxious from not knowing what to do, how to communicate or how to find his way home that we didn't want to go near him. My dad never smiled during this time. He was always angry. He became depressed, and the way he treated us reflected how he felt. Sadness, depression, fear, and anxiety dominated our lives.

We were not allowed to make noise or express our own fears as children. We were not allowed to complain. We found ourselves suddenly subjected to more rules than back in Lebanon, which I didn't think was even possible.

As a child, I didn't understand the extent of my father's suffering. Looking back, I see that he went from having a good job in an environment where he felt important to a new country where he couldn't communicate and could barely earn an income to support his family. It must have been difficult, because his dreams were shattered as well, but at the time I didn't think of his pain. My siblings and I were too busy drowning in our own misery to pay attention to what our father was going through.

After a few months, my parents were able to rent a small apartment in a very poor neighborhood. My siblings and I were registered in school, and we started adapting to our new environment. We lived in such poverty that the local church donated used clothes to wear and dirty mattresses to sleep on. I was forced to wear a thin, ugly blue coat that I was teased about constantly at school. I could feel the cold winter in my bones because the coat was not warm enough. In those days, nothing was easy or simple—every breath required effort.

We realized then that there were not going to be any horses.

One Piece of Feta Cheese

I hated waking up and I hated sleeping, because sleeping meant waking up the next day and going to school. I had to find a way to integrate into my new culture and adapt to both school and peer pressure. Unfortunately, I was failing miserably!

My classmates saw me as ugly because I didn't look like them, stupid because I didn't speak their language, and dirty because... well, I don't know why, because I really was not dirty, but they kept saying that I stank. All the kids would run away rather than be close to me—except when they were beating me. At every recess, a different group of kids would be waiting for me; they took turns because it was such a fun activity to torture the girl who didn't belong or fit in.

The kids were creative: One day they would just hit me all at once, other times they would dig a hole in the snow and bury me in it. At times, they would practice spitting on me, and sometimes they would compete to see who could punch me the hardest. Despite how hard I tried to avoid recess—the school rules didn't allow me to hide in the classroom—I simply had to endure the beatings *every single day*.

What about the teachers? Well, you have to remember that I couldn't communicate in English (and neither could my parents, so if they had been asked to come to school for a meeting, they wouldn't have been able to communicate either!). Teachers would ask me a question, and I would struggle to understand. This frustrated the teachers and made me feel like a burden on them. Sometimes I felt as if they wished I weren't in their classes. Most of the time, I wished to be unseen. I learned to adapted in order to survive.

One day when I was in class, the teacher sat down in her chair only to suddenly jump up. When she realized that she had sat on an egg, she was furious. She said something to the students that I didn't understand. They all pointed at me, and I still didn't understand. The teacher looked at me and said something that I also didn't understand, but it was clear that I needed to answer her. I had no idea what to say, but I reasoned that a *yes* would be better than a *no*, since it symbolizes acceptance and compliance—the opposite of confrontation. When I innocently said "yes," she looked at me with fury and asked me to leave the class. That's when I realized that I had admitted to placing the egg on her chair.

I am sure each of my siblings went through similar experiences, but we didn't discuss these things—or much of anything, for that matter. None of us wanted to talk about what we were going through. Our priority was to learn English, and we did that by watching TV and studying—yes, studying in a language we didn't understand! The pressure to always be studying was so intense that I disconnected from my siblings. I actually have little memory of a relationship with them during this time. I am sure my brothers and sister were going through the same pain, but we never really connected to ease each other's suffering.

You see, while my parents worried about survival and basic physiological needs, along with financial strain and integration challenges, they also still worried about their reputations. And the more fearful and stressed my parents became, the more pressure I was subjected to. My parents became stricter. They ensured that I didn't escape our cultural traditions, which meant there was a whole list of things I was not allowed to do. I was not allowed to have friends outside of the school environment—going out with them was totally forbidden—not that this would have been an easy task, considering that I was not accepted by anyone I knew, and I didn't understand—but I badly wanted to have a friend.

I was totally alone. It seemed to me that what I was going through was so unimportant compared to what my parents were enduring, so I just accepted my new life. I just had to survive this stage of my life until I started high school. I dreamed of growing up and becoming stronger—not so that I could fight back, just so I would be able to endure the beating.

Despite how little we had, my mom tried to make our experience bearable with her creative cooking. With the depleted energy she had in her hard life, she would introduce us to new dishes every week. She managed to infuse our meals with love in her effort to make us feel better, which we did, sharing these great moments eating together. (To this day, we still talk about some of those signature dishes—and we laugh because they definitely don't taste as good now as we felt they did back then!)

We didn't always have enough to eat, though. One time, I came home from school feeling hungry, so I opened the fridge and saw just one piece of feta cheese. I looked at it and couldn't figure out how four kids were going to feed off this small piece of cheese. So I decided to show God how good I was and did not eat anything. That night, I went to bed hungry. But something interesting happened. The next day, as I ate, I felt very thankful that we had food. This feeling of gratitude not only made the food taste better, it made me realize that things were not so bad. The hunger I felt the day before made me appreciate food when I did have access to it. I realized that no matter how difficult my life was, or how many things I felt I didn't have, I still had privilege—the privilege of filling my belly. (To this day, when I eat, I enjoy and am grateful for every bite!)

The first year in Canada was dominated by sadness and fear of the unknown. But it ended with something amazing: My mother gave birth to my baby brother, and I felt such immense love for him. Having a baby in our family brought love to our lives and alleviated the pain of our home environment. The handful of happy memories I have from this time include holding my baby brother tight to my heart because it felt so good, also the closeness we had with our mother—and, of course, her amazing cooking.

My Best Friend

High school presented me with a great opportunity: new classmates and a new environment. Plus, I now spoke English and French, so it was easier for me to communicate and fit in. I saw it as a fresh start, a new beginning where my odds of being accepted would be higher, and this was exciting to me.

Making friends was much easier in high school, though, truthfully, I just wanted to go unnoticed, to live my days without beatings or humiliations. Nevertheless, a great thing happened in high school: I met my best friend. She was the first kind person I had encountered since I arrived in Canada. She was a Lebanese girl who seemed at ease with Canada and had Canadian friends, so she was accepted by everyone. After my parents met and approved of her, for the first time since I arrived in this country, I was permitted to hang out and do activities with a friend outside of school. Our time together was filled with laughter and joy, and I started looking forward to going to school for the first time. I now had a close friend whom I trusted and loved! My new friendship offered me a lot of strength, along with some much-needed breathing space.

This new friendship and my status as a high-school student suddenly afforded me lots of opportunities for social outings: I got invited to friend gatherings, to the movies with classmates, to school events. Guess what my parents said? They responded very firmly that I was not allowed to participate in any social activities: no going to the movies or out with friends, no school trips or dances. I couldn't do any activity outside school hours. Why? Because a "good girl" does not do these things without great risk of bringing shame onto the family.

As I turned fifteen and my dad no longer saw me as a child; his hugs and laughter had stopped long ago. In his eyes—or perhaps in society's eyes—my growing up highlighted certain risks for him.

My dad's perception of women was influenced by his inherited social norms. He grew up thinking that it is the duty of fathers to shelter and protect their daughters, and of husbands to shelter and protect their wives. Women needed to be protected from themselves. They should not be allowed to think freely. Doing so would trigger ambitions that might become a problem, because, as women seek to fulfill their ambitions, they might do something that would bring dishonor upon the men in the family. It seemed I was doomed to go from one hell to another. I felt controlled and suffocated again. I started feeling hostile toward my parents.

I convinced myself that, despite the fact that my dad kept the pressure on me, things were better because at least I was not getting bullied. At least I had a real friend whose company I enjoyed. Once again, I decided to accept my circumstances, be grateful for the things I did have, and start dreaming of becoming free in a couple of years, when I would finish high school and start university.

The most pleasure I got at this stage of my life was when I was dreaming. I would take advantage of every minute to visualize what I would become when I graduated from high school and started college. I saw myself strong. I imagined getting a degree from a university and working. I dreamed of being financially independent so I could be free.

Then one day my father surprised me with the news that the situation in Lebanon was getting better and that the civil war was in its last stages (or so he thought). He decided that we would leave Canada and that I would finish high school in Lebanon.

I was devastated. I went to bed crying. I started remembering what life was like when I was growing up in Lebanon: the social pressure, the rules, the suppression, the gap between the life I was dreaming of and the possibility of ever achieving that life in my home country. I felt that I would be returning to the jail I left when I was a little girl, only now it would be harder, because I was a young woman, which posed a far greater threat to my father and his reputation.

The thought that I would have to integrate into a new community and meet new people was exhausting to me. I had already struggled to integrate in Canada, and just as I was beginning to feel a sense of belonging, I was being forced to leave it all and return to a place I didn't know anymore, a homeland consumed by rules and limitations—especially for women!

I felt bitter. I couldn't eat, couldn't think, and was consumed with trying to come up with logical reasons that would make my father reconsider his decision. I even asked God to make my dad change his mind. Was this another of God's tests? If it was, I truly wanted to be spared. For the first time, I was just too tired, and I asked God to stop testing me.

But eventually I realized that this was my destiny. I had no choice but to accept it. As the date of our departure grew near, I cried and cried and cried.

Death Was All Around

We arrived in Lebanon to find relatives living in our three-bedroom home. Despite the fact that my father had informed them of our return to Lebanon, they refused to vacate. My father decided to be patient rather than aggressive with these family members. His patience meant that we would live in a one-room apartment on the ground floor of *our* home until they agreed to leave.

Two adults, five kids, and twelve boxes of clothes and personal items in a space so tiny that we had to remove our mattresses from the floor every morning just to be able to walk around. Worse yet, every week I watched these relatives leave for *their* main apartment in Beirut and return to live in *our* house on the weekends. Yes, these people used our home as a mountain getaway while we suffered. Misery!

To add insult to injury, we were again subjected to Lebanon's historical problems, regular electricity interruptions, no drinking water, and nothing that enabled the comfort of simple day-to-day living. We lived in this situation for more than three months, until finally my dad convinced the relatives to vacate our house without any hard feelings.

I used to wonder why my dad was so tolerant and why he took such care in avoiding any hard feelings. As an adult, I now understand that his behavior was simply part of the social norms to which he had adapted. Socially, he didn't want to be perceived as intolerant toward relatives, so that he could maintain the respect of his community. He wanted to be perceived as a "good guy" who would not fight with relatives—even if it meant his family suffered.

Moving back into our big house made us more comfortable logistically, but life in Lebanon was not an easy ride. I compared everything about my lifestyle in Lebanon to what I'd had in Canada. In Canada, no matter how poor you are, you still have access to clean water, electricity, and heat. These basic human needs, I realized, were luxuries in Lebanon. In our house, we could only heat one room. The more I compared, the more I struggled to adapt; I just couldn't understand why we came back.

Lebanon presented me with a totally new lifestyle, whereby basic conveniences required effort. For example, to take a bath, first we needed to ensure that we had enough water. Then we needed to place the water in a pot, heat it up, and carry it to the bathroom. Having access to drinking water took effort because we had to go out and fill up gallon containers ourselves, and then we had to monitor how much we drank because we didn't want to run out. Everything required effort. Sadly, even today, people living in certain areas of Lebanon still struggle to meet these basic physiological needs.

A few months later, when school started, my dad decided to send me to a public high school. This meant taking courses in Arabic—a language I hadn't studied since I was eight years old. Reading was a struggle, learning was a struggle, understanding how to behave was a struggle. Fortunately, my mom dedicated herself to helping me and my siblings study the Arabic language. We were her only priority, and her commitment to us was instrumental in helping us adapt and pass our courses.

We humans are gifted with an amazing ability to adapt. And that's what my family did. Once again, in the span of a few months, we had adapted to the suffering. We reacquired the Arabic language, integrated into school, and started feeling a sense of belonging.

I became very popular at school, since the Lebanese love people who are "international" and speak different languages. To them, I was a beautiful Canadian with curly blonde hair. Everyone wanted to be my friend, including boys, and I loved it! I started liking school again, and I enjoyed my friends. I even enjoyed the attention of boys, but I knew I had to be cautious around them—and I was. I was very careful not to engage with them too much—just occasional conversations here and there. Things were slowly starting to feel on track.

But being popular created more issues for me, or rather for my dad. Remember how I explained that the most important thing for my dad and his social environment was honor? And remember everything my dad did to ensure the utmost respect from relatives and friends? I knew that one simple, unintentional misstep from me could dishonor my father and bring grave shame onto him. That is why I was always very careful with my speech and actions.

One day, I came home from school, and my father greeted me with an expression full of anger. I was terrified. In my mind, I immediately started playing back all of my recent actions, desperately searching to see if I had done anything that could be considered "wrong." He looked at me with extreme hostility and told me to follow him to the living room. I felt my legs weaken so much that I couldn't believe they could carry me into the next room. My father shut the door behind us.

He asked abruptly, "Who did you talk to today?"

I couldn't even comprehend the question. Who did I talk to? My teachers? My friends? Then it dawned on me whom he was inquiring about.

"I did not talk to any boys," I said honestly.

He went on to tell me that one of his respected relatives had visited to inform him that my reputation was at risk because I was seen talking to a girl who was suspected of having a boyfriend.

"Are you friends with her? Do you talk to her? How much time have you been spending with her?" His facial expressions made me feel as if talking to this girl had been a severe crime. I was confused. And I had to be very careful: I had no way of knowing whether what I was being asked to admit to was a punishable offense.

The shock on my face must have made my father realize that he should explain: "If you want to hurt a man, throw a bad rumor around his honor. It doesn't matter to me if what they're saying about your friend is true or false, but I will not allow my daughter's honor to be affected by this girl's reputation."

Honor, what? I had simply been talking to a girl who was accused of having a boyfriend. And that was my grave crime? What?

My father went on to tell me the story of a very honorable man who lived in our village. This man told his daughter to take poison and commit suicide because he found out that she loved a man. She "loved" him because she had been seen *talking* to him.

I got so scared that I couldn't feel my legs. I was terrified. I thought I had known the rules, but clearly I had not; there was a whole new dimension of rules that I couldn't even grasp.

That night, I went to bed feeling totally confused. If I didn't understand the rules, I might break them without meaning to. Regardless, the consequences would obviously be severe. I was, however, very clear on one important point: My father considered my death a much better option than allowing me to dishonor him.

The next morning, my father spoke further to make sure that I understood he truly loved me and that the pressure he was placing on me was for my own good—so I could stay safe and the family's honor would remain intact. He made it very clear that, not only should I not talk to boys, but also not talk to girls who talk to boys.

Planning my life around these conditions seemed somewhat challenging. I didn't want to break any rules, though; I just wanted to survive this phase of my life. I knew I had to adapt and manage the situation. So I started ensuring that my father knew my friends and approved of them. This was my way of reducing the risk of having friends that could be perceived as dangerous to my reputation. I also shared my every emotion with my mother, and she acted as my guide to safety. I reasoned that if she knew everything I was doing, she would certainly flag any risky moves I might make.

The school year finished in June, and on the last day of school war erupted again. Only this time, it was close to home: The civil war reached the village where we lived, and I now experienced the ugliness of war firsthand. Suddenly, my whole environment was about death, attacks, danger, bombings. My friendships were shattered as families retreated to different geographical areas in search of safety and we lost track of each other. Of the friends who stayed, I witnessed many of them dying. My dreams of going to university were reduced to just wanting the violence to stop. We just wanted to stay alive.

My father decided to send my big brother back to Canada in an effort to prevent his involvement in violence. Saying goodbye to him was immensely sad because we didn't know if we would see each other again.

We were living one moment at a time, with no visibility of the day ahead. It was hard, so hard, so painful. We would move to one house, and within a couple of weeks, the area would become dangerous, so we would have to move again and find shelter from the violence. There was no way to predict which areas were safe or for how long they would remain safe. At one point, we had to live with another family because there weren't enough apartments to rent; this lack of privacy added a new challenge to our lives as we struggled to tolerate each other's habits amidst a civil war.

A weekly newspaper would announce the names of people killed in the week's skirmishes, and every week I would look to see if there were any I recognized—and I always found some. Death was all around. The only thing I wanted was for my parents, my siblings, and me to be safe. I didn't want to die yet.

This went on for several months—until the situation became unbearable and my father decided that we would go back to Canada. Again, the airport was closed, and again, we had to go through another country, this time Jordan. Again, we suffered the exhaustion of finding airline tickets, waiting for long periods at the airport, and fearing the unknown that was waiting for us in Canada. But this time we had one saving grace: My big brother was already there, so at least we would be staying with someone we loved and missed terribly. My dream of hugging him and feeling safe was the only thing that kept me going.

The moment we boarded the plane in Jordan, I took a big breath and finally felt safe. I relaxed my body and rested my mind.

Girls Don't Need to Attend University

When we arrived in Ottawa, my brother was there, waiting for us. It felt so wonderful to hug him. Although my brother's two-bedroom apartment was a little small for seven people, it didn't matter—we had water, electricity, and the basic conveniences to make us comfortable. There was a beautiful tree across the street from his apartment, and I would go outside on his balcony and just smell the air and feel exhilarated that we were safe and given a chance at a new beginning. We could start fresh in a city that was familiar to us. We knew the system, we spoke English, and we had everything we needed to be happy. I felt no worries or fear looking upon that beautiful tree, and I was confident that a great future was waiting for me in Canada.

I was now seventeen. I had finished high school and was ready to start exploring universities in Ottawa! I wanted to become a lawyer, and I began planning in my mind the steps to achieve this dream. Since universities are cheaper for Canadians, and I was a Canadian, I could take out a student loan so I would not be a burden on my father. I would study and get my degree, and I would defend every victim. I was going to contribute to making the world a better place. I was going to end racism and discrimination. I was going to spread caring, fairness, empathy, and love. I was going to spread the importance of dreaming and freedom.

I saw no obstacles; I had no worries. I was at peace. The difficult journey was over, and I was now on a fresh new page. I was getting closer to my big dream of becoming productive, financially independent, and free. All the difficulties I had ever been through would be worth it—because I was going to go to university and become a lawyer.

One morning, I got out of bed and decided to take the first step toward becoming a lawyer: I would visit a few universities to gather information about the application process and requirements. As I was getting ready to leave, my father asked where I was going. I explained to him my plan for the day.

My father looked at me in surprise. "Why would you go check universities? You don't need to go to a university. You need to look for a job."

I looked at him in shock. *Why would I look for a job?* I thought. I am not qualified for a good job, and I don't have the education needed to start a good career. What kind of a job would I get as a high school graduate?

His face mirrored my expression. He was shocked that I would have even the slightest thought of going to a university.

"Girls don't need to go to university" he explained carefully, "because they will eventually be married to someone who will earn the income and take care of them. Besides, you have responsibilities here. It's much more important for your brothers to get an education because they need to provide for their future families."

My eyes felt as if they had popped out of my head. I couldn't relate to a word he was saying. I started explaining to him that if I had a law degree, I could help the family a lot more than I could with a high school diploma.

He responded, "You always want to revolt. Why can't you accept who you are? Why are you always challenging our ways?"

I argued, of course, but he quickly interrupted by handing me the newspaper and saying, "Look for a job. You will not be going to university. End of discussion."

Barely able to stay upright in the middle of our kitchen, looking at my father's stern face and my mother's helpless expression, I saw my future-self flash before my eyes: I saw myself old and tired, with no dreams. I felt like I was a prisoner again, with no hope of being free. When would the suffering end? How would it end? I was numb. I couldn't understand why any father would do this to his own daughter.

Was it possible that he just didn't love me?

With time, I realized that he did love me and that he was programmed to be this way. He was simply behaving in alignment with his social background. My father believed that girls should not get a higher education, because that's what his culture taught him. He believed that girls should be controlled so that the reputation of the family would not be risked in any way, because that's what his family had taught him. Later, I came to understand that I didn't really factor into his decisions—his upbringing did. I was just in the way. And, over time, I no longer blamed him for that.

On that morning, my world collapsed around me. I felt as if I had just received *another* life sentence. For the first time in my life, I questioned if I would be able to find a positive opportunity out of another hardship. I wondered why God was doing this to me. I had never done anything wrong—never even told small white lies—so why was God doing this to me?

But despite feeling ready to give up, the next day I started calling to set up interviews for jobs listed in the newspaper.

While I was making calls, my father came to me and explained, "You are my daughter and I want what's best for you. You will secure your future when you marry a good man."

I looked at him with total disappointment as he continued, "Your priority now is to find a job and help your family. It's more important for your brothers to get an education."

It wasn't until much, much later that I recognized an even bigger tragedy than my father disallowing me from getting a higher education—even bigger than him being a victim of society. The real colossal tragedy was that he deprived himself of freely loving his daughter and supporting her dreams, because society programmed him to focus on managing the risks of having a daughter instead of enjoying a relationship with her.

At times I was so depressed that I didn't want to find a job. Other times, I hoped I couldn't find one so I'd be forced to get an education! But the truth before me was irrefutable: I had to find a job. I had to accept this new reality.

So, I decided to find my light. I decided to turn this sad milestone in my life into an opportunity. I started talking to God, asking for help. I did this constantly because the thought of never having an education and never having a career was unbearable. With my dream demolished, I needed God to help me. I decided to make a deal: I promised God that I would be good, and in return, I asked him to help me through this hard situation. This gave me hope; I trusted that God would deliver.

Chapter 2

My Career

It didn't take me long to find work. My first job was with an investigation company, where I became a typist. My daily tasks were to listen to audio reports recorded by investigators and to transcribe them. I also produced formal investigations reports. I hated the work, but I learned to type eighty words per minute and discovered that I was an excellent, hardworking employee. I decided to focus all my energy on my new job, and my dream became to learn as much as possible and take on more responsibilities.

Why did I care to learn more about a job I hated? Well, I realized that learning was the only thing that no one could take away from me. I reasoned that if I could excel at what I was doing, I could have success—and then I would be able to leave that job to do something more interesting. Don't you feel confident when you excel at something? I needed to feel confident that I was learning *something*.

I also realized that the less I knew about my job, the harder it was to do my tasks. But the more I knew, the more I was in control and the easier the tasks became. With this great revelation, I realized that I was in control of what and how much I learned—there were no limits to learning—that it was all up to me.

The Branch Manager

Have you ever experienced how new information can free you from difficulties? For example, before you learned to ride a bicycle, it probably seemed really difficult to do. But when you learned how to do it, it became enjoyable, right? This notion applies to everything in life. When I discovered the magic of learning, I started feeling exhilarated; I started becoming stronger. Being knowledgeable meant that I had things to talk about, I had an opinion. I started perceiving learning as my new door to freedom and independence—and I became an information addict!

My new state of mind changed how I felt about life. I was now excited to understand what the company I worked for did. I understood the importance of my job, and I felt useful. I became consumed with working full-time to earn a living. I wanted to prove that I could be a professional and an adult, even though I was a very innocent seventeen-year-old girl.

I would arrive at work earlier than anyone else and leave after everyone else—mostly because the only bus-pass I could afford after giving all my earnings to my father was the cheapest one, which was only valid during off-peak hours. It was cold waiting for the bus, especially when the temperature would drop to -22 degrees Fahrenheit (-30 degrees Celsius). I immersed myself in my job; I wasted no time and skipped lunch breaks. Because my time was saturated with work, and because I also didn't have a personal life, I was very good at preserving the family honor!

My manager was a man in his thirties, and I noticed that he stared at me in a way that made me uncomfortable. Remember, I was not allowed to talk to boys my own age, so the thought of interacting with a grown man really frightened me. Every day, he would get closer to me, which was terrifying. I felt unsafe, and I didn't know how to behave, so I would just focus on typing. I rarely spoke; even if he made comments about my work, I wouldn't engage in conversation with him. If he spoke to me, I would respond in the briefest possible way, usually with either "Good morning", "Thank you", "Yes", or "No."

One day, he walked over to me as I was typing. He stood, watching me type, and then he touched my long braid. My thoughts immediately started racing: *Why is he touching my hair? What does he want to do to me? There is no one here to protect me!* His touch made me feel dirty, and I hated his presence. It felt like abuse. It felt disgusting. It felt scary! I believed that I was in danger, and I was terrified.

I couldn't talk to anyone about this; I had to ensure that my dad would never find out—I didn't trust his reaction. And I couldn't leave my job, because my father would ask why and I could never lie to him. There were two colleagues at work who were kind to me, but we kept our distance, and I didn't feel comfortable telling them. I was feeling disgusted, scared, and stuck. So I did the only thing I could do: I prayed and asked for help. It was all I did. I was either working or praying, day after day.

But my manager would not stop. He became more and more frustrated with my lack of response, until one day he decided to make things clear. He gave me two choices: Either I would go out with him (and I had no idea what that meant) or he would report me to the head office to get me fired. I didn't respond, hoping he would just leave me alone. But every day became worse than the day before; he was getting pushier and pushier. I just kept working and refused to react.

Then, one morning, an older man from the head office came to visit our branch for a couple of weeks. He set up in the conference room across from my desk, facing me. For two weeks, he watched me day in and day out, without ever saying a word to me. Yet I felt a sense of security with him being there. His subtle gestures made me feel safe, and there was no bad will in his calm eyes and kind face. I said good morning to him when I walked into the office and goodbye when I left. And not once during this time was I alone with my manager. I loved it! Because the older man's presence somehow made the manager stop talking to me, I wanted him to stay forever. I felt so safe and so grateful to God, because, the way I saw it, God had heard my prayers and sent someone to protect me.

At the end of the second week, the older man called me into the conference room and introduced himself as the owner of the company. He looked at me compassionately as he told me that he had come to the branch to fire me based on multiple reports the manager had submitted describing me as someone who was not committed, who needed supervision to work, and who was a below-average employee in general. He went on to tell me that the manager's insistence on firing me raised his suspicions, especially since I was a junior employee and could not have been solely responsible for the underperformance of the branch, which my manager had attributed to me.

The man went on to say that he had decided to visit our branch to see exactly what was happening, to understand the real reasons behind this branch's underperformance. He said that, as he watched me work, he realized that I was the hardest-working employee there. In fact, he decided that I deserved to be promoted, not fired!

I felt both an amazing sense of relief and an immense sense of gratitude toward God. It was as if God were telling me, "I told you I am here... This was a test and you passed it." From that moment on, I became more committed than ever to passing every test God threw my way; the intensity of my joy was beyond any happiness I had ever felt before. I was so proud of myself, and I felt very secure that the relationship I had with God was real and solid.

The owner explained that he wanted to promote me to branch manager. Moreover, he would give me the authority to fire the current branch manager—the man who had been harassing me!

Let's stop for a moment, because this is when I had to define who I was. This offer felt like a second test. I wasn't sure how I knew this, but deep inside I felt as if God were testing me again, and I was determined to pass all my tests. I wondered, *am I an ethical person? Am I someone who would enjoy vengeance? What is the professional thing to do? What shows strength of character? More importantly, what would God want me to do?* All these questions went through my mind within seconds, and I immediately knew what I had to do.

As the owner of the company started to suggest that I take

time to think about his offer, I responded: "Sir, I have no interest in firing anyone, or taking his job. If I am to be promoted, there needs to be a vacancy, and currently there is no vacancy."

I felt great. I felt strong. I felt confident. I loved *me* for not taking the opportunity for retribution. My decision solidified for me that I was a good person, and I decided that I would use every opportunity presented to me to strengthen the goodness inside me. I would never allow anyone or any situation to drive me to become bitter or have negative feelings.

The president of the company was shocked. I left the meeting not knowing what he would do, and frankly, I didn't care. Breaking free from my worries made me feel strong; and for the first time since I started working at the company, I felt more powerful than the manager. I didn't care whether he stayed on as manager or not, because the next time he tried to intimidate me, I would be ready to put him in his place. He would no longer pose a threat to me.

A few weeks later, my boss was let go and I was promoted. I didn't ask any questions; I simply took on the added responsibilities. At seventeen, I became the branch manager. I poured my energy and my passion into my new job.

I trusted God more and more, because he seemed to be delivering. In my relationship with God, I felt safe and strong.

Going to Night School

Eventually, I left the company for a better job, and from there I had one success after another with different companies. The more I succeeded, the harder I worked and the more I learned. By the time

I turned twenty-one years old, I was already a national manager responsible for multiple outlets across the country.

Despite my new job title, life was still hard financially, given that my salary had to support a family of seven. My father was working as a taxi driver—his degree was not recognized in Canada, and it was too difficult for him to learn a new language and start over. He was very unhappy. His dream was to save money and relocate our family to Lebanon when the war ended. So my father's dream became my next test: Support my family financially until we could return to Lebanon. This was an easy test that I knew I could pass, because I already felt it was my responsibility to contribute to the collective life of my family that I loved so much.

With time, I became a strong professional woman and felt very secure about my status; I was targeted for recruitment by important companies. But even still, something was missing: a college degree. I craved learning new things, and I knew that no matter how smart I was, I needed higher-level training to be able to evolve. Back then, there was no Internet, and access to knowledge came only from a formal education.

My performance was impeccable, to the degree that my employer was willing to fund my education. I was thrilled. I felt like my life was finally coming together, that I was on my way to pursuing my dreams again. There was just one little problem: *How would I fit in work* and *college?* At the time, night programs were very limited and not offered by all reputable universities. *What kind of education would I be able to get, given that it had to be a night program?* I searched and searched for a window of hope—I was willing to take anything.

Finally, I found a night college program to study business administration. Without even thinking about it, I enrolled and entered a new phase of my life. Every day, I would leave home at 6:00 in the morning, stay at the office until my class started, go to college straight from work, and then return home at 11:00 p.m.

My college degree took eight years to complete, but during those years I was continuing to rise through the professional ranks. I was getting promoted faster than any of my colleagues—so much so that anytime I would be transferred; my boss at the new branch would resign, announcing that he or she would not be able to compete with me so it was better to get out of the way! My employers expressed fascination at my level of output. I received awards for my performance, and I became a benchmark for success.

All of these events were clear evidence to me that I was simply passing my tests and God was rewarding me. I never got carried away with the events themselves or the people around me. I attributed my success to my relationship with God.

The Perfect Life

But despite the fact that my work achievements compensated for my hardships and made me stronger, I was unhappy. As a young woman in her twenties, I started missing not having a personal relationship. I wanted to love and be loved. I wanted to go out to parties, I wanted to socialize. But I couldn't have a personal life without inflicting pain on my parents—all of these activities were still forbidden. Dating was against our cultural values, and just a mention of the idea of marrying someone from outside our culture would devastate my parents. I couldn't bear to be a source of pain and dishonor for them, because despite the social restraints that felt shackled to my ankles, I loved them. To me, they were loving parents, and I couldn't handle the guilt I would feel if I harmed them by ruining their reputations. So I refrained from any social activity.

To comfort myself, I allowed myself to dream of the love I might share with a boy (now a man) I knew from my childhood. This was the same boy I had fantasized about as a little girl. Ghassan was the son of my parents' long-time friends, and I remembered him as strong and gentle, despite the fact that our childhood relationship amounted to me (at six) dreaming about him (at sixteen), and him not noticing me! From the time I was six years old, I had never stopped dreaming of him.

Part of the reason I was attracted to him was because he had a great relationship with his father, a relationship I craved and had never actually experienced. I admired Ghassan's dad so much that I wished I could have him in my life. I reasoned that it was the closest thing to having a loving relationship with my own father. Maybe marrying into this family could give me an alternative to what I was missing.

Every night when I went to bed, I wondered about Ghassan, despite the fact that he was basically just a fantasy. The fantasy felt good, though, and it was enough for me in terms of a personal life. In fact, I used to wear a ring and tell everyone that I was engaged, so that no one dared get close to me. But this lie eventually had to end because no one can be engaged for that many years.

My relationship with my dad was becoming more intense because I was independent now. If I arrived home late from the office, my father would be angry and hostile with me. On the weekend, if I suggested we all go to the park, he would get upset and refuse to join us. My financial independence and ability to plan activities for my mom and siblings made him feel no longer in control. He was in pain. Things got so intense between us that we didn't speak to each other most of the time, and when we did speak, we would argue. It got to the point where he and I couldn't be together in the same room.

I felt empathy for my father. He believed that he lost everything leaving his country for Canada, and this made him very unhappy. But my mom was always there compensating with her love. She did everything she could to make our family happy: She would prepare maté, a tea that's drunk through a small straw, when I arrived home from work, and we'd all sit and share the moment. She would tell us stories about Lebanon. She made sure that we never forgot the Arabic language.

I looked forward to being with my mom and my siblings. I used to think that we had a perfect life because we loved each other so much. So why couldn't my father be happy? What more did he want? Why was it so difficult for him to integrate socially in Canada? Why wasn't he able to let go of the past and start living in the present? No matter how hard I tried to reason with him, no matter how hard I tried to show him the opportunities we had, I couldn't change his emotions or state of mind. He was stuck in a past that he liked and couldn't enjoy what he had in the present.

You might be wondering why I didn't walk away from all of it, especially now that I could. The reason is that, to me, the situation was another test of my faith. I loved my siblings so much that I could never leave them before they became independent. I was a source of comfort for them. I looked at my mom and siblings as if they were all my children, and I did everything I could to keep them comfortable.

A year later, I was offered a promotion in Toronto, where I would have to live on my own. I wanted the job and some distance from the unhappy environment in our home. But how was I going to leave my mom and my siblings? I confided in my mother, and she said that if I needed a break from all of it, she had no objections to me taking the job. Her approval gave me comfort, and I decided to accept the offer.

Darkness in Toronto

Toronto was crowded and booming. It was difficult to find an apartment, so I had to rent a basement in a three-story house. Scant sunlight came through the windows, which impacted my emotional state of mind.

On my first day of work, I met my boss, who turned out to be arrogant, egocentric, and just ordered everyone around. This attitude made his team unhappy, which affected the overall environment. The work itself was all right, but having a boss who hides the macro view of the company took away from the pleasure of working.

Nearly every day after work, I would go home and call my mom. Most of the time, our phone calls included her telling me how much she wanted me to come back. We would both cry. Every weekend I would drive to Ottawa. Seeing my mom and siblings was amazing, but my dad was always unhappy, and he would become hostile around me. I didn't understand why. Was it because I left?

The three years I spent in Toronto were the hardest I had ever experienced: I was unhappy. I missed my mother. I didn't like my job. I didn't like the city. The people I met at work and in town were mostly unhappy and complained about financial difficulties and complicated relationships. I seemed to be surrounded by the negative energy of everyone's messy lives.

But what really made this time of my life worse than previous times was the amount of guilt I was feeling—for leaving my mom and my siblings, for no longer being able to protect them from my father's negative emotions, and for no longer being able to take them out, laugh with them, share stories with them—because I was no longer there.

There I was, finally, totally independent, with the opportunity to build the life I wanted, and yet the darkness surrounding me affected my outlook on life. I couldn't enjoy my freedom.

But three things kept me going: my relationship with my mother, dreaming of a man I barely knew, and connecting with my God. The harder life got, the more comfort I found in strengthening my connection to God. The connection felt good because I trusted it, and I saw every heartache and obstacle as an opportunity for something better. Any time things would get hard, I would say to myself: *It's only a test. It will pass. Just stay positive and you will get through it the same way you have all your life.* Over the years, I had observed that my life seemed to work this way: at the end of every difficult experience, there would be a nice one—as if it were my reward for staying the course through difficult times. Noticing this pattern cemented my faith in God and validated my belief in my power to make good choices.

The Scent of Flowers

I rarely took a day off from work. But on this particular day, I couldn't bring myself to go to the office. I stayed home, and as I laid on the couch in my living room, I fell asleep and began to dream. In my dream, I saw Ghassan, the man I dreamed about every night, taking my hand and walking me out onto a balcony. Then the balcony turned into a beautiful garden. Everything felt so real. I felt that I was with this person; I could vividly see the entire garden and smell the scent of the flowers.

Suddenly, I woke up to the sound of my doorbell. It was my friend coming to check in on me. She walked in and said, "Oh, your living room smells like flowers!" I looked at her with fascination. I certainly had not sprayed anything with a flowery scent. So what was she smelling? Surely, she wasn't referring to the scent in my dream. Is that even possible?

I chose not to analyze this curious event any further. I simply trusted what I felt in my gut: this was a direct message from God that great things were waiting for me if I had the strength to break free from the negative environment in which I was living. I decided on that day that I would leave Toronto, return home to Ottawa, and start a new relationship with my dad. The next day,

I moved back home.

Because unmarried people living alone isn't acceptable in my culture, getting my own apartment in Ottawa was not feasible—I wasn't trying to start another war with my father. In fact, I had returned home with a different perspective: I recognized that I was independent and no longer needed my dad, but maybe he needed me. Instead of expecting him to act like a father and treat me with love and support, I decided to approach him without any expectations and deal with him empathetically. I decided to understand him and comfort him. I decided that I wouldn't allow any tension in our family home. I decided to try to make him feel safe—in other words, to assure him that I wasn't going to ruin his reputation.

I was no longer ready for a fight. I was no longer blaming him or on the defensive with him. I had zero expectations for him. When my dad was stressed, I simply avoided being around him. When there was an opportunity to participate in pleasant conversation, I engaged him. I don't know if it was my peaceful attitude or if other factors impacted my dad's demeanor, but things were calmer with him. Things were all right.

My relationship with my mother grew stronger too. I could talk to her about anything. We would go out daily after I came home from work, whether to a mall or to shop for food. Our relationship was full of joy and laughter. Peace infused our household for the first time, and it was good for my siblings as well. We all got by with the least amount of tension and things became acceptable.

As I got older, my desire to be in a serious relationship grew. I was also being pressured by my parents to accept arranged marriage proposals, now that I was in my twenties. It was customary in my culture to marry within the same community, a critical factor for both my parents. My marrying outside the community would be devastating to them and their reputations, and would subject them to harsh judgments from their family and social circle. It would also mean that I'd be disowned. And not being able to see my mother was simply too big of a risk. Furthermore, marrying someone my father approved of would ensure lasting peace between us, because my threat to his reputation would simply cease to exist; there would no longer be any threat of dishonor.

The pressure for an arranged marriage became so intense that I finally told my mother, "If I were to marry anyone from my community, it's only going to be Ghassan." Yes, her best friend's son and the man I dreamed of every night. I had no idea if he was married; I didn't know what he was doing. I knew absolutely nothing about him. All I knew was that he was the man I had dreamed of marrying since I was a girl! I confided in my mom that I already loved him—had loved him for many years—and that I had a deep feeling that he wanted me as much as I wanted him. In my heart, I believed that we were perfect for each other.

My mother was worried that I might be putting my life on hold waiting for a dream to materialize—a dream that she felt was an illusion. She loved Ghassan and his family, but how could I love him without knowing him any better than a stranger? Although my mother was hoping my feelings for Ghassan were real—because she would be thrilled to have him as her son-in-law—she was pretty certain that my feelings for him were *not* real, and that if I saw the *real* him, I'd see how little we had in common. Although our families were best friends, Ghassan and I were from two different worlds: I grew up in Canada and was not open to adapting to rigid social rules; Ghassan grew up in Lebanon, which meant he would likely share my father's priority of social conformity.

My mother was trying to protect me from experiencing in marriage the same social pressure that my father imposed on me. She wanted me to find someone whose life principles were aligned with my aspirations. But since I was insistent that Ghassan was the one, my mother concluded that I should meet him. She decided that we would travel to Lebanon for a few days, visit with friends and relatives, and enjoy the country; we'd also fit in a brief visit with my parents' best friends. My mother figured that once I met Ghassan, my childish fantasy would shatter. I'd get him out of my system and could pursue a more fitting husband.

I was excited to go on vacation to Lebanon and finally see my dream man! I had been fantasizing about this guy my whole life. And you know what? I had this intense feeling that he loved me back and had been waiting for me all this time too! Yet, I had to remind myself that all these emotions were in my head. Besides, I rationalized, we hardly knew each other. He was ten years my senior, and the odds of him already being married were high. What if I got to his house and saw him sitting next to his wife? What if he had kids? Or what if he was single but was nothing like the man I had been dreaming about?

I could feel my anxiety rising. I was nearing a critical

moment in my life. You see, not only was I potentially stepping into a life-changing marriage, I was also potentially ending my long-standing dream. Fantasizing about Ghassan gave me something to look forward to every day—what would happen to me once the dream was over?

The way I saw it, the dream would either come true and become a joyful reality, or it would be revealed as a lie, crushing my hope.

I pulled myself together and convinced myself to stop thinking about it. I would just take things moment by moment. Because, as much as I was worried, I had a deep feeling that he wanted me as much as I wanted him. Beneath my worries, I believed that my dream was about to become a reality.

My Dream Guy

Once in Lebanon, my parents and I spent a few days touring and enjoying friends and relatives. Two days before we were set to return to Canada, we headed to Ghassan's home. While the meeting was planned on our end, it wasn't totally scheduled: the social norm between friends dictated that we not call and arrange the visit ahead of time. Also, phones were not common in that part of the world at that time.

My heart was beating fast from the moment I awoke that morning. I was excited and scared at the same time. After a forty-five-minute drive, we finally arrived at their house. We all got out of the car, and I stood behind my mom like a shy toddler hiding from a stranger. I started visualizing Ghassan sitting next to his wife, with his kids around him. . . . Then I shook these thoughts from my head and pulled myself together, of course calling on God to help me through whatever I was going to experience in the next few moments.

I walked up two flights of stairs behind my parents, my heart pounding and my face reddening. I felt as if I were going to faint! I was either getting closer to the manifestation of my life's dream or the end of it. I kept talking to God and asking him to help me through this.

When I reached the top of the stairs, there he was. He looked exactly how I had pictured him, sitting with his family on their front terrace. The moment I saw Ghassan's face, and before either of us said a word, I realized that he had been waiting for me. His eyes were filled with love and passion. He smiled as if he were saying, "Finally, you came." Even his family had a look of relief, as if, finally, the time had come—for what, I didn't know, but I suspected it might have something to do with us finally getting together.

It turned out that he was getting pressured to marry as well, and he had expressed to his family that he was waiting for me. His parents, like my own, had been impatiently waiting for our reunion so that they'd put an end to this fantasy: We'd either get over our silly dream or make the dream come true.

His family invited us to spend the night at their house, and my parents agreed. I was ecstatic—I didn't want to leave! That evening, even after our respective families had turned in for the night, Ghassan and I stayed up talking. He told me that he had noticed me when I was in my teens, after we had returned to Lebanon. He thought that I was a good-looking, intelligent girl, and he hadn't been able to stop thinking about me since.

He said that, over all these years, he couldn't help but think of me. He would wake up early every morning, sit, drink his coffee, and visualize me. He pictured me going to work. He imagined us together, enjoying each other. In his mind, we already belonged to each other. This revelation astounded me. Because, while he was dreaming of me each morning from Lebanon, I was dreaming of him each night from Canada—at the exact same time! Were we connecting energetically? Were we visualizing our dream to be together despite the fact that we were not physically in a relationship? Whatever it was, I promise you that it was more powerful than any physical experience would have ever been.

That night, we talked and talked and talked, as if we had always known each other. It was as if all the time we had spent together in our minds was time that we had really, physically, spent together—that's how comfortable we felt with each other.

At some point in the evening, Ghassan looked at me and said, "So are we going to get married? I think we wasted enough years."

You might be thinking, *What?!* I know how crazy this proposal sounds. We didn't even know each other! Plus, I lived in Canada and he lived in Lebanon. Where would we live? How would we live? How would any of this work? It's true that I had never really interacted with him before—at least not in the physical sense—but because I had been dreaming about him most of my life, I felt that I knew him—perhaps energetically.

I looked at him with incredible love and immediately said yes! I was ready to leave everything to be with him. I felt as if this amazing dream were materializing in front of me. I didn't want to analyze what was happening; I just wanted to bask in the pleasure of the moment. I started thanking God, because there he was rewarding me again, and this time it was a huge reward: It was a life of happiness!

When our families woke up the next day, Ghassan ran to his father to tell him to ask my father for my hand in marriage; it's customary for the father of the groom to be the one to approach the father of the bride-to-be with a marriage proposal. Meanwhile, I ran to my mother to tell her that he had asked me to marry him and I had said yes. Both families simply said, "Finally!"

My father and mother were thrilled. I could immediately see the relief on my dad's face. It was as if, in that brief moment, a heavy weight was lifted from his shoulders, a weight shaped by his worries about me—who I would marry, if I would marry, how his social circle would judge my life and my decisions, how this judgment would affect the respect he was accorded. . . . I realized just how exhausting that weight must have been for him.

I started feeling my dad's love for me in that instant. It was as if the weight of his fears and worries had held captive his love for me. When the weight was lifted, I could see love in his eyes again, love I hadn't seen since I was a child. For the first time, I was flying with joy: Not only was my dad happy with this marriage, I was going to marry my dream man!

From the moment my father learned I was engaged, he changed the way he treated me. He even hugged me—yes, he hugged me, something he hadn't done since I was a small child—the morning of our engagement. As he hugged me, I didn't know what to do. I didn't know if I should hug him hard or just keep it light. I wanted to cry, but I figured it would probably make things uncomfortable and emotional for both of us. And I was confused: How could all the hostility disappear in the blink of an eye? Just because I was no longer a threat to his honor? His hug was quick, but it felt amazing.

I realized that my father had been living in defense mode all his life, and his perception of the threat I represented as an independent woman triggered a lot of his hostility and "unfair" decisions toward me. The social pressure was so intense that it brought out the worst in him and nearly devastated him. When I was no longer a threat to his social standing, he put his guard down and went back to being my dad. One part of me felt terribly guilty that I had put so much weight on his shoulders, while another part felt happy because I now realized that my dad loved me, something I had questioned most of my life.

This hug was a milestone in my life. Although it didn't become a habit, it broke the walls between us and made it possible for me to hug my dad every now and then!

I spent two days with my new fiancé, and then my parents and I headed back to Canada—where I initiated Ghassan's visa, which took about ten months to be processed. At the time, phone calls were not possible between Lebanon and Canada except from certain outlets in the country, so on weekends Ghassan would drive about thirty miles (forty-five kilometers) to an outlet that allowed international calls. A lot of times we had to speak with a third person on the line. It wasn't fun having monitored calls, but at least we heard each other's voices. I lived for the weekends just to hear him. We also wrote beautiful, expressive letters to each other. Ghassan is French educated and, at the time, didn't speak or write English; I only knew how to write Arabic conversationally. Still, even though it wasn't proper Arabic, it was enough for him to understand me.

This was a beautiful time for me. Not only was I constantly thinking of my fiancé, such as imagining what our first hug at the airport would feel like, I was each day closer to fulfilling my dream of getting married to him.

On top of that, I had a real father again. Free from social pressures, my father was finally relaxed. He became calmer, and he no longer pressured me.

Total Inner Peace

One day, as I was sitting in my office, I received a call from Canadian immigration telling me that Ghassan's visa was ready. Oh my God, what a moment! I ran to go pick it up, and I immediately mailed it to him. He received it, bought an airline ticket, packed up, and, a few days later, landed in Canada. My dad and I went to the airport to pick him up, and the hug felt as great as it did in my dreams!

A couple of weeks after he arrived, Ghassan and I had a small wedding ceremony. During the celebration dinner I started feeling worried. *What if this doesn't work out? What if it's better in my dreams?* The more questions I had, the more worried I got. But when I looked at Ghassan, and our eyes met, I totally surrendered to joy. All that mattered was that I was married to the man I had dreamed of all my life, ever since I was six years old.

After the ceremony, Ghassan and I traveled for two weeks. I wanted to show him how beautiful Canada was; together, we went to Quebec City and Niagara Falls.

The most pivotal part of this whole experience was the feelings that Ghassan triggered in me. First, there was total inner peace. I felt safe; I felt loved. Everything was just so enjoyable. And there was also something very deep that Ghassan gave me: the need to forgive anyone who had ever hurt me, intentionally or not.

You see, when you feel the intensity of love that I felt, there is no room for anger, no room for hate. When you get this taste of love, you just don't want to feel anything else, because nothing compares. I was (and remain to be) so in love that I chose not to feel anything negative. I started feeling empathy toward people who had been unkind to me—and the more love I felt, the more empathetic I was. I forgave the kids who bullied me; I forgave the manager who harassed me. I was able to let go of all the negative baggage because the love I was carrying was simply much more enjoyable.

And I believed that I owed it to God to let go of all the unkind events that had happened in my life. I had been rewarded with love, and I wanted nothing else. My marriage was the beginning of a new life, one full of joy and peace. I felt such gratitude for this relationship that it changed my outlook on life.

Two years into my marriage I became pregnant. The exhilaration of my pregnancy was beyond any excitement I had ever felt.

The moment my son was born, I was cemented in a sphere of love and gratitude. On that day, I also met the father in Ghassan, and I fell in love with this side of him. As I watched the tender way he comforted our child when he was hurt, got down on all fours to play with him for hours, or patiently put him to sleep at the end of a long day, I would become overwhelmed by the amount of love and security Ghassan bestowed on our little family. Part of me secretly wished I could have experienced as a child even a small fraction of the affection he showered our baby with.

On the career front, I continued to do very well. And because I was happier in my personal life, I became more balanced and my professional achievements grew. I used the love I had in my relationship to fuel my work. I found solutions to problems and always ensured my team was performing at its peak. I had the reputation of being a strong businesswoman in addition to being an excellent manager—I loved managing people. I was strict but kind. I was supportive and very compassionate. I was famous for motivating people toward productivity, always keeping the best interests of the company as my number-one priority. In fact, I once received an award for increasing production from 300 to 1,200 units without adding any employees or using extra time. I advanced again and again. I became renowned for outstanding achievement.

I was in my twenties, at the top of my game . . . and yet I was starting to get bored with my professional life. I knew my job so well that work had become a routine, offering nothing more to discover. I was simply using my knowledge and experience to produce. I began to feel like a robot—just going through the motions to get things done. Although I was well-compensated for my job, I lost the excitement of going to work every day.

Though I was really good at what I did, I had started to feel that something was missing. I would meet people who talked about things that I didn't understand and realize I wanted to learn more. I wasn't sure what new field I should learn about, but I knew that what I was doing was not all there was. This feeling was accentuated when I read about MBAs and higher degrees. I started to realize that my college degree was primitive and that there was more out there I should aim for.

Is This Who I Am?

One day, the company I worked for announced that we had to cut overhead costs. And as one of the senior managers, I had to make critical decisions. I knew exactly who I needed to fire to achieve my department's cost-cutting objective. It wasn't a hard decision, because I knew it was in the company's best interest.

And so, on Christmas Eve, I fired Heather with the calm and efficiency I brought to so many other tasks. As I told my employee the news, I watched her expression turn from shock to disgust. Her green eyes filled with tears, but she didn't allow them to trickle down her cheeks. Heather didn't say a word, but her eyes spoke volumes. Her look of disgust jolted me like ice water thrown on my face.

As I spoke to Heather, a voice in my head asked me, *Couldn't you have waited until after Christmas?* I immediately started wondering, *Yes, why didn't I wait until after Christmas?* But I knew why. You see, I was so focused on my job—on productivity and output—that I forgot about the people. I didn't think about my employee's very human reaction to being fired, or about how the decision would affect her life. I didn't think about her family. All I thought about was that *I* wanted to get this done before Christmas so *I* could meet my objective, so *I* could go home and celebrate the holiday. I didn't see Heather as a person; I saw her as a number that I had to reduce from my overhead cost. For the first time in my life, instead of being happy about successfully executing a company objective, I felt bad.

After that day, I wondered: *Is this who I am?* I was so trained to robotically meet one business objective after another that I lost my humanity. I was so entrenched in ensuring financial security for myself, so focused on producing excellence at the business level, that I became disconnected from my feelings as a human being.

Firing Heather on Christmas Eve gave me back my soul. And being in love and enjoying a happy personal life gave me the motivation to get more out of my professional life. It had become crystal clear to me that behaving like an emotionless robot was robbing me of my potential. You see, I had been trained to ensure a positive impact on a company's bottom line, without realizing that I could—and perhaps should—strive to have a positive impact on people.

With this new dimension in my thinking now activated, I decided that I needed to fill the hole in my heart with love—love toward the people with whom I worked, love toward any living thing with which I came into contact. I wanted to be human again; I wanted my passion back. Most important, I truly believed that I could continue to succeed while preserving my humanity—I didn't need to choose one or the other.

I decided to shift my career to the management consulting industry; I saw it as a place where I could add value to sustain institutions made up of groups of people. I applied to all the firms in this developing field, but I was attracted to a boutique consulting company known for its special touch—it believed in developing its consultants and investing in them both professionally and personally. This company believed that for people to provide effective consultancy to clients, they needed to be at peace, to be evolved on the personal level. The company valued learning and sharing, and believed that investing in the personal growth of its consultants gave them wisdom and increased the quality of their services. This was attractive to me, so I applied for a job.

I Was Nothing

But as always, I ran into obstacles. I was a woman in a man's world, and I didn't have an MBA from a reputable university. All I really had was my experience, so I was rejected. But I was so determined and so sure of my own skills that I offered to volunteer my services for free. I reasoned that if they saw how committed I was they would recruit me. My husband supported my decision, despite the fact that I was sacrificing my income. He had faith in my abilities and knew that I was striving to evolve personally. And the company accepted my offer!

Guess what happened? I immediately realized how little I knew. All the big-headed feelings I had because I was a big shot at my last company were broken into pieces when I realized that there was a world of knowledge that I was missing. I felt very insecure. I knew next to nothing. I was nothing.

Do you think I let my shattered ego stand in my way? No! I let my feelings of not being good enough drive me to read books, to interact with others, to listen and think. I was finally learning again; I learned so much that volunteering my time was well worth it. I discovered the beauty of working with people instead of just managing people to achieve objectives. Learning made me feel valuable. I was so happy to have my mind expanded that I forgot I was working for free.

Within a few months, I proved my excellence. In fact, I was ranked the highest in terms of customer satisfaction, which was a critical measure, given that I was now a consultant who delivered services to customers. My performance shocked the owners of the company. My high customer-satisfaction ranking triggered more business, including repeat business, and within a few more months I was a revenue-generating consultant—still working for free!

Six months from my start date, the owners recruited me officially. But for some reason, my financial package was 50 percent less than my male colleague, who, by the way, had less experience. Was it because I was a woman? It seemed every phase of my life introduced me to a new type of unfairness: racism, harassment, and now gender discrimination? I saw this as another opportunity to define who I was. I had to decide how to deal with this situation and whether it was going to make me feel bitter or provide me with another opportunity for growth.

The thought process was easy. I made a simple pros and cons

table guided by my personal objective. There were two paths I could take. The first one was to ignore that I was being paid less than my colleague and instead show my value. I (perhaps naively) believed that no company would underpay someone they viewed as valuable. Plus, I believed that God was watching over me, and my history with God had shown me that if I focused on positive emotions and doing the right thing, I would be rewarded.

The other option was to demand fairness in the package. This might trigger hostility within the company, and they might view me as being too much trouble or too demanding, at a time when they had not seen my full value yet.

So which path would I take?

I decided to ignore the fact that I was being underpaid and instead recognize that this was *my* path. I was not going to let a detail, like a deficit in salary, deter me. I firmly believed that in time I would show how much value I could bring to the company, and then the income would correct itself. And I trusted that God would guide me.

I began working full-time and loved it. There were a lot of opportunities to learn, and the people were high-quality; I felt enriched by the presence of such high-caliber consultants. I made great friends and excelled in my job.

Remember how I wrote that I felt like I was nothing? Believe it or not, I still felt that way. When the ego I had developed based on my previous professional successes was destroyed, the ego weight was lifted off my shoulders. The incredible feeling of being nothing made me feel clean. My mind was being detoxified. In that space,

I began to feel as if I were no more important than anyone else. I recognized that there was a universe of knowledge that was waiting for me to discover it. And I had a constant hunger for learning.

As I earned credibility for my job performance, I knew that I had to find a way to strengthen my academic background. I explored getting an MBA, but I didn't have the academic requirements. Then I discovered a management consultant certification program. This credible certification was not common but was valued by the company I worked for; they encouraged all their consultants to get certified.

Given my professional reputation, I was accepted into a three-year program. I was exempted from certain courses, but I still had to take the exams. Three years later, I became the only certified management consultant in the company, yet I was still earning 50 percent less than the male consultants, despite my stronger professional experience!

I was convinced that eventually God would trigger corrective measures, as he had done before. I was not going to allow unequal treatment to bring negativity into my life. I believed that everything would happen in due time.

I was on track, happy, and thriving professionally. But I still felt academically inadequate. So I searched for a credible part-time MBA program, now that my experience, professional reputation, and certification merited a stronger chance of being accepted into one.

And I got accepted!

The program was challenging, but it didn't slow me down. You see, I was determined to be an outstanding professional, an exemplary student, a great wife, *and* a perfect mom. I felt that I shouldn't have to sacrifice any of these roles. Fortunately, my husband's support made it possible to be all these things without any compromises. He did things that men in my culture simply will not do, from helping me prepare our food and setting the table to tidying up the house and hand-drying dishes.

As a family, we readjusted our priorities. We gave up our social life and gym membership. I studied when my son went to sleep. Usually Ghassan would be sitting next to me, drinking Yerba Mate and doing his own reading. I would share what I was learning and he would listen with interest. He revered this powerful side of me. Sometimes, when I was so tired I could barely see straight, Ghassan would massage my shoulders as I finished an assignment. The more committed to education I was, the more he supported me. And the more he supported me, the more grateful and loving I was. It was a beautiful cycle. For the six years it took to complete my MBA, he carried me and kept me strong.

Two years into the program, we had another baby. I'll be honest: I didn't think it was possible to feel more love. But when our second son arrived, I could feel an outpouring of love from three directions: from me, from my husband, and from my firstborn. I was overwhelmed with emotions. Watching the love my four-year-old felt for his baby brother was unlike anything else. He would play with the baby, wipe food off his mouth, and sing to him if he was crying. Our older son basically cared for his brother the same way his dad and I cared for him.

My drive to learn was increasing. I believed that getting an education would help me be a better wife and mother. The more I learned, the more I became addicted to learning. Then one day I was given the chance to evolve as a consultant. Instead of managing consulting projects, I would develop the methodologies. This is when I delved into research. I coupled my research findings with my professional experience, and I developed a methodology that places people at the center of organizational change. I loved the enlightenment I achieved through this process. My state of mind would constantly shift, from focusing on the goals of the organization and looking at people as tools to focusing on people and recognizing that they would pour their hearts and souls into the organization to achieve what was in the best interests of both the organization and themselves.

An Urge to Leave

My contribution to the company was increasing day by day. I became such a strong revenue driver that I was promoted to a senior manager position at the firm. This was an amazing achievement. To reach this level of seniority in such a company was something to be proud of!

Let's hold still for a moment and reflect on where I started. Do you remember the seventeen-year-old typist? Now I was a senior manager in a consulting firm!

But something major happened when I reached this stage. While I had a strong feeling of joy for receiving the promotion, I suddenly didn't want to be a part of the company anymore. I felt like I was being drawn away, as if God were guiding me toward a different path. You see, my husband enabled me to feel a deep sense of inner peace, and that, coupled with my longtime connection with God, became an unmatched force in my decision-making process. I felt emboldened to go with what felt right, and this company didn't feel right anymore. The feeling was intense, like an urgent warning to leave before something bad happens. There were no logical reasons for this feeling. I just needed to leave.

At the same time, I began having the urge to return to Lebanon. This feeling was also more spiritual than logical—and it certainly was not realistic, because my husband and I would have to leave our jobs, relocate, find work, and settle, all of which were huge unknowns.

But all I could think about was that it was time to return to my home country. Ghassan believed so much in my relationship with God and my gut feelings that he supported me with great confidence. I felt as if I were receiving a calling to go on a new mission, a mission that could impact people who could benefit from my knowledge and experience. I felt that it was time to share what I had learned and to influence more people positively, and I sensed that Lebanon was the place to do this.

Lebanon had just come out of war at the time. The country had barely anything in terms of infrastructure, advanced technologies, and so forth. While our living situation would be challenging, the crippled state of the country meant that I'd have the opportunity to make a great contribution. I discussed this with my husband, who believed God and my intuition guided me to make the right decisions. He said, "We have nothing to lose and everything to gain. . . . Worst-case scenario, we can always come back."

Another perk of going back to Lebanon was being closer to my husband's father. I had dared to dream about the possibility of experiencing a meaningful and loving relationship with my father-in-law, a relationship that I hoped might compensate for the deficient one I had with my dad.

So, it was decided. Everyone thought I was crazy to leave all that I had worked so hard for, and to take such a huge risk as moving to Lebanon. But the message from my heart was far more powerful. I had no expectations. I just had an intense feeling that I needed to be in Lebanon, to be open about what was ahead, and to make big contributions. So I left my company, packed up, and moved our little family to Lebanon.

Interestingly, I found out a short time afterward that the company I had worked for had gone bankrupt. Was this the reason behind the urgent feeling to leave it? Maybe. All I knew was that this was God's way: You receive messages to go in a certain direction. You don't know why, but you go in that direction anyway. And then, time eventually shows you that the new direction was in your best interest all along.

Chapter 3

Back in Lebanon

My husband and I arrived to a country that was recovering from a civil war. The infrastructure was dreadful, roads were treacherous, electricity was unstable, and clean water was inaccessible. Getting settled was difficult. And integrating into this new society was hell—I felt like a total outsider. Although I understood the culture, I didn't feel comfortable living in the environment. I had difficulty understanding the social customs, but more important, I had difficulty accepting them. Small things like receiving visitors without the visit being prearranged were difficult to adopt, and individual privacy was simply not respected.

I was faced with having to submit to doing the "right" things all over again. Only this time, I was a mature, independent adult. I wasn't going to conform, but I was going to make it work.

Success at Work

I focused on the positive things I did have; for one, a relationship with my father-in-law. I enjoyed being part of my husband's family and being close to Ghassan's father. I also focused on trying to establish myself in Lebanon and experiencing life in this beautiful country.

I got a great job where I launched the consulting services of one of the top four firms in the world; the job gave me the security I needed to succeed in this country. My Lebanese heritage, coupled with my Canadian experience and my now-strong educational background, helped me in creating the needed methodology for Lebanese organizations seeking to leverage their culture and transform it to support their goals rather than fight their culture and view it as an obstacle.

Within weeks in this company, I became a success story. I used techniques that were totally foreign to the Lebanese way of working, such as connecting intimately with people and involving them in the changes their organizations were making. I discovered the immense pleasure of interacting with others, positively influencing them, and learning from these activities—and I excelled at these things. I loved contributing to improving people's lives.

My work was appreciated by both my employer and customers. Within a few months, I became well-known for my ethics and for creating win-win situations. I also became renowned for sharing knowledge and instituting a practice of learning within the companies with which I worked. Most importantly, I became famous for managing change and transforming culture in organizations, at a time when change was constant and extremely painful, even for organizations.

The recognition I received for being good at helping organizations transform made me want to alleviate the pain directly, instead of just recommending how to do so. The more I saw people suffering from being treated like robots, from being conditioned to produce without any regard for their mental well-being, the more I saw an opportunity to trigger evolution—personal evolution and social evolution. I saw the great potential of launching that transformation in the workplace, since that's where many people spend most of their time.

But I felt limited in my scope of theorizing, analyzing, and making recommendations. I realized that I was no longer satisfied with just counseling work—rather, I wanted to do what needed to be done. I was very familiar with the pain caused by change—I had experienced so much suffering in my life because of change, and also the lack of it. I knew that people could be very resistant to trying new things, especially when change called for bold transformations. But I wanted to prove that change could be an exhilarating process, that it could trigger learning and evolution. I knew exactly how to achieve this. I wanted to be part of the implementation process. I wanted to be involved in the implementation of my recommendations.

Spiritual Nourishment

At this point in my life, I had a regular practice of caring for both my physical and spiritual dimensions. I took care of my soul by allowing myself to feel love, connecting with God, and experiencing a sense of belonging. I called this practice my *spiritual nourishment*. I took care of my body by exercising and nourishing my body with clean food.

I decided that I wanted to bring spiritual nourishment to the workplace. I believed that if I could trigger evolution inside an organization, I could trigger evolution in society—because the people that form these organizations also form society. I got hungry for an opportunity to start this journey of implementation, and as usual, God responded.

I was managing an interesting project for a client—a large institution in Lebanon—when a man, after seeing what I was able to do for the institution, offered me a senior position to run his company. I was exhilarated! I instantly knew this was an amazing opportunity to demonstrate all that I had learned over the years.

The business owner gave me full support, committed to a no-interference strategy, and allowed me the authority to do what needed to be done to move his organization toward international excellence. I found myself working with a businessman with ethics, someone who trusted and respected me, and who gave me the space I needed to evolve his company.

I was filled with gratitude for the task before me. I also felt an intense responsibility to prove that organizations could treat people as spiritual beings instead of robots. If I could prove that changing our leadership style could activate passion and reflection, and also trigger love and learning, inside organizations, then I could prove this could be done for the rest of the country.

This journey was not easy, because people were not accustomed to operating in such an environment, but it was very successful. The company tripled in size in a short time, became known for its resilience, and earned the recognition of the international community by consistently achieving credible awards.

The realization of the power I had and my decision to use this power to create a healthy environment that supports people and activates their minds, while at the same time ensures discipline and respect for company policies, was exhilarating for me. My position helped me positively influence people. I realized that infusing an environment with love can trigger respect for policies and procedures, not because people are afraid of being fired but because people want reciprocated love; they will go the extra mile to protect an environment that nourishes their soul.

Chapter 4

A Journey to Wake Up

My relationship with God seemed to be paying off, and I was confident that I understood exactly how this world works. I believed: *I am good, so God is good to me.* I figured the deal was that if I stayed good, God would never let anything bad happen to me or allow me to suffer.

Hello, Universe

Then one day, two years after returning to Lebanon, my father-in-law passed away, suddenly. I was devastated. Losing him turned my world upside down. For the first time in my life, I had been enjoying a special relationship with someone who was like a father to me. How could God take him away? Why take him if I hadn't done anything wrong?

You see, not only did God take away a loved one, he took away the foundation of my belief system. Losing someone I loved deeply confused me so much that I started doubting if God was actually there. Because how could he do this to me if I had behaved so well?

The more I doubted God's existence, the worse I felt. This

experience threw me into confusion, leading me to have severe panic attacks for months. I constantly questioned: *Did God exist? Or was my relationship with God the output of my imagination? Did I create this God in my mind because it was the only way I could cope with the hardships of my life?*

The idea that there might not be a God terrified me because, frankly, given what I had been through, I didn't trust humankind. To believe that there was no God controlling the cruelty and greed of people horrified me. I had to be on medication for almost a year, and during these months I didn't feel good. I was tired, and I had memory gaps; my brain power was incapacitated. I couldn't innovate. Most important, I couldn't dream. I was beginning to feel like an emotionless robot again. My passion was depleted and my physical power was drained. Learning was simply impossible!

By this time, I had two children I adored, and I needed to get back up on my feet for them. How could I help them through life if I was devastated? It was my duty to get better. I had been well-trained to do whatever was necessary to be there for others, and this time it was for my children, so I had to find a solution.

My reason to evolve was love.

And so, my search for spiritual truth began. I was driven by a decision I'd made to never be a cause of stress to my children. I wanted to be their friend and their mother. I wanted to provide them with love and security. To do this, I needed to establish a new foundation for my relationship with God. And, therefore, I needed to comprehend how God worked—I needed to understand the universe. My research was underway.

The first thing I realized was that I had been wrong to believe in a punishment-and-reward relationship with God. It no longer made sense to me that the God I had experienced operated on a system of punishments over love and guidance. As I searched for more answers and for the truth, I correlated my personal experiences with acts of God; I linked my behaviors and attitudes with manifestations. I tracked key events in my life that I had perceived as negatives, only to recognize that they were positives—for my own good.

The more I explored my own life events, the more I realized that I had a love relationship with God. I discovered that God had given me things without expectation and that he carried me and supported me in a powerful way when I was weak. This could therefore not be a punitive relationship.

The more I reflected on my life and on my relationship with God, the more I realized that I needed to reset my belief system. I needed to wipe out all the tenets engraved in my mind by society and establish a new belief system that was more aligned with my personal experiences.

I used one scale to help me validate my new belief system. It was a simple scale: If the belief system triggered any negative emotions, it simply could not be true, and certainly was not reflective of God. If, however, it prompted positive emotions, then it certainly was about God. For example, if I believe that God punishes, then my behavior would be driven by fear of punishment; this brings up negative emotions, and it simply cannot be true. If I see God as the source of love, this means that the more I love, the more I am cherishing God; this inspires positive emotions and, in my new belief system, it is the truth.

This process helped me to detox the foundation of my spiritual beliefs; it allowed me to shift from seeing God as doling out rewards and punishments to seeing him as pure, unconditional love. I shifted my thinking from fearing God to loving and trusting God, and I became ready to receive any guidance made available to me to understand this reality.

Being ready to receive meant that I carried no negative emotions. I forgave all the cruelty I had been subjected to, and I allowed myself to have a new, clean belief system, free from biases and judgments. In this new state of receptiveness, I sensed that I would soon experience some kind of event that would give me a chance to reboot my belief systems and start on a new spiritual journey. I just needed to be patient.

From then on, I became very aware of signs that I would receive. I began to call "God"—the only God I had ever known—"the Universe," which, in my mind, encompassed unity with every living thing. I shifted my thinking from *religion*, which divides people into groups based on ideology, to *oneness*, which is inclusive of everyone, regardless of ideology. Oneness is driven by a common foundation of love!

And with this new state of mind, I started living life with more awareness.

Signs from the Universe

I woke up one morning with this strong feeling in my gut that I should get a mammogram, despite the fact that I was in my thirties and had no symptoms or physical evidence of illness. I just had this strong, un-ignorable feeling that I needed to get tested.

When I visited the doctor, he recommended that I wait. He said, "Nahla, you're too young, and there are no indicators that would suggest that a mammogram is necessary."

But after leaving the doctor's office, I began to receive what I interpreted as physical signs that I must do the test: I met someone who had survived breast cancer due to detecting it early; while driving I saw billboards for the early detection of breast cancer; and while conversing with someone, the topic of breast cancer popped up out of nowhere. These signs, coupled with my gut feeling, increased my sense of urgency to get a mammogram.

So I insisted on the test. And the results came back quickly, stating that everything was normal. I didn't believe the results. I walked out of the lab and went straight to the hospital and had the mammogram redone. This time the results were not ready as fast. Fifteen days later, the hospital called and asked me to come in to discuss the test results with the doctor.

On a Wednesday in February, the doctor explained that the pathology took longer than expected because what they found was uncommon—they needed to be sure, and now they were sure. I was diagnosed with pre-cancer!

Pre-cancer meant that whatever I had was going to *become* cancer, it was just a matter of time, one doctor told me directly. How was that possible? Despite having had many logical reasons for *not* having the test done, it had proved I had a serious situation on my hands. Had I postponed the test, as my doctor suggested, I might have eventually been diagnosed with full-blown breast cancer.

My first reaction was fear. I thought of my children. *What will they do if I die?* I thought of my husband. Then I did what I have always done when faced with a difficult situation: I connected with the Universe. As I was accustomed to doing, I asked for guidance. In that second, when my thoughts shifted from fear to acceptance and trust, I was flooded with gratitude. I became so grateful that it was pre-cancer, not cancer.

I was also grateful for the experience of having trusted my gut and noticing the physical signs. The more I reflected on how I was inspired to do the examination without any concrete evidence of illness, the more I was convinced that there was a power guiding me all along. The more I thought of the correlation, the more I trusted and the more I accepted—and my doubts disappeared. How could I possibly be afraid when I had the power of the Universe supporting me?

For a moment, I felt a bit of shame—here was this power triggering me and guiding me every step of my life, and there I was afraid and doubting. I had no reason to feel this way. So I moved into a state of inner peace, total acceptance. I had total trust that I would not face this pre-cancer alone. The power of the Universe would surround me, and I was convinced that things would work out just fine.

That moment marked me. I felt very lucky. I believed it was the beginning of the inner cleansing that I had sensed was coming and that I felt I needed. I suspected that this experience might be my fresh new start, and so I began connecting with the Universe with immense gratitude. And the more I felt gratitude, the less I felt fear. I decided that I would do everything I could to get better, all the while surrendering to the power of the Universe and trusting it. This was going to be a test of my newfound relationship with the Universe.

No, I wasn't making a deal with the Universe. I wasn't agreeing to be good and stay the course so that the Universe, in turn, would keep me healthy. I was simply making a commitment to do my best and trust that the Universe had a master plan. This power that had guided me all my life had never let go of me—and I reckoned that it wouldn't this time either. I would learn to surrender.

I immediately decided with tremendous confidence that I wanted this pre-cancer cut out of my body. So as the doctor was telling me about the options available to me—"We can try radiation... Or we can do nothing and see what happens," he offered—I stopped him and said that I wanted to remove the pre-cancerous cells surgically. The doctor looked at me a bit bewilderedly.

"Doctor," I pleaded gently, "removing that area of my body would cure me, right?"

"Well, yes, it would actually be a cure, . . . but I can't make such a drastic recommendation to someone your age," he replied.

Do you think I listened to his advice? No. I felt so strongly that surgery was the right thing to do that I scheduled it for Friday that same week, two days after my diagnosis.

I immediately started receiving strong messages from the Universe about what I would be going through after the surgery. I communicated the messages to my husband to prepare him. I told him that I would end up having multiple operations and that I would not fully recover before June, three months later.

Rather than feeling worried and afraid, I felt protected, as if I were being cuddled by a beautiful, soft, fluffy cloud of love. I felt so comfortable, so in control, and so close to the Universal power, that I somehow knew I wouldn't suffer during this long process. I actually felt safe!

As the messages I was receiving started to materialize, I trusted the Universe more and more. As I predicted, I had multiple operations: one time the hospital made a mistake in how they installed the tubes, and another time I had a complication from an adverse reaction to antibiotics; these operations would trigger more operations.

One day, I really tested my relationship with the Universe when I had to make a quick, tough decision: Go through an operation using local anesthesia (because I had eaten that morning) and likely feel the pain of the incision or wait a full day to do the operation with general anesthesia on an empty stomach? The operation was a real emergency. What was I going to do?

I had to decide how much I trusted the Universe. I reasoned that if I could do this, then I would never doubt again. And since the repercussions of not doing the operation were severe, I decided to trust the Universe and do it the same day.

As I was being prepared for the operation, and during the whole process, I repeatedly called to the Universe. I wanted to show my high trust in the Universe, and I also desperately wanted to feel comforted by the Universe, knowing I was being watched over. I was clinging to the Universe the whole time, my awareness focused solely on it, asking for help. And before I knew it, the operation was over. I had felt no pain, and there I was in a state of total trust!

While I was in the hospital room recovering, doctors in training would come to my room to review my case because it was unique. I had taken a chance with the operation, which had been experimental; the doctor's approach was uncommon, and there was no scientific evidence that it would actually solve the issue, but there were no expected side effects apart from discomfort afterward. The staff wanted me to be realistic and understand that this operation might not solve the issue I was having. One particular doctor looked at me squarely and said, "Please prepare yourself that this will not lead to your recovery."

I shifted my attention to my husband, who was by now used to receiving my prophetic messages, and simply said, "I will be fully recovered in June."

And, in fact, in June I was fully recovered. I did it! Against doctors' predictions, I had prevailed. I had felt nothing but love as I went through the hospitalizations and operations. I truly did not feel pain. What I went through defied medical science and logic.

But it wasn't only about recovering, it was about spiritual evolution. How could I have gone through this experience and have any doubt about how the Universe works? Saying that it had been a great test of my faith is an understatement!

My days from that moment were filled with gratitude and joy. My external environment and outside circumstances had little impact on how I felt—my inner-self now controlled my feelings.

My deep gratitude was so much stronger than pain, so much stronger than fear! I felt gratitude for being alive, for receiving the Universe's messages, for having the courage to act on those messages.

This experience also taught me about acceptance and surrender, which have been among the greatest gifts of my life. The feelings of surrender and acceptance, for me, led to incredible feelings of peace and serenity. I finally felt safe, an amazing sensation that freed me from fear.

You see, the ability to surrender after doing everything within our control stems from a recognition of what we *can* control and what we *cannot*. It rises from accepting that we're only able to do so much. When we can accept our limitations and put trust in the Universe, we open the door to freeing ourselves from fear and anxiety.

As I mentioned, before this health crisis I had begun to question how I saw God and my beliefs about him. But going through this experience, as I had anticipated, solidified that my thinking about religion and God had not been entirely accurate. My outlook had changed. I no longer saw God as a man sitting up in the sky, monitoring my behavior, and punishing or rewarding me. I now saw God as unconditional love, a power that is waiting for us to reach out to it. And when we do, there is no suffering—we begin to be guided to love, to gratitude, and to surrender.

I now fully believed in the Universe and in the oneness of living things. I had trusted the Universe, and I came out of the ordeal no longer doubting its power. Seeing the big picture—understanding the power of the Universe and the power of our thoughts, and how connected we are to each other and to the Universe—made me feel certain that we are powerful, we are magical, and we control our destiny.

With this realization, I found my next calling: sharing with others what I had learned about how the Universe works. I truly believed that if people could understand how powerful our connection to the Universe is, there would be less suffering. I already knew that I could convince others that personal evolution was possible, because it had happened to my husband, who was a core witness to the magic that we experienced as a family. I reasoned that if I couldn't help others in easing their pain and finding their paths, then what was the purpose of everything I'd gone through? What was the value of my experience?

I needed to find a way to share what I had learned. But this did not turn out to be an issue. Because in conversations with my friends, managers, employees, and even people I didn't know, the topic would somehow drift to personal issues and solicitations for my advice. Individuals just started coming to me to talk about their problems, their challenges, their worries, and their anxieties. This gave me the opportunity to talk to them, to share my story, to introduce the Universe to them. They listened as I explained the life principles I had discovered, such as acceptance, gratitude, connection, and the importance of dreaming. They enjoyed our conversations and were touched by what I said, and they would usually feel better afterward.

Yet, while I found myself comforting people during times of suffering, and also preaching and giving advice, few individuals would take steps to make lasting changes to their perspectives and lifestyles. Very few would actually make the effort to establish a connection with the Universe. This lack of willingness to implement my recommendations became frustrating to me.

After a couple of years in this mode, I grew tired of preaching, and I grew tired of people failing to apply these concepts to their day-to-day lives. I still wanted to share my story, but I didn't want to be in a position where I imposed myself on others. That's when I had another realization: It was not my job to push people but rather to assist them when they were ready and asked for help.

My life taught me that people need to be ready to search for their own truths. People make changes or act on their own timelines—they cannot be rushed. All I can do is have my part of the truth accessible to them when they're open to listening. This notion prompted me to write down what I've learned for the people in my life who I wanted to impact the most: my children. So, I started to write this book. I wanted to make my knowledge available to them if and when they became ready and needed it. I didn't want to pressure them into diving in before they were ready. The lessons I learned and principles I followed would be a handbook for them, a guide to follow when they were ready to listen.

After completing my first draft, I realized that writing solely for my children was limiting the reach of my story. I always dreamed big—so why not share my story with anyone who needs it, when they need it? I reasoned that maybe my words could help others validate their own perceptions and their own experiences, or help them as they carve their own paths in life.

I decided I was ready to share my life's lessons with the world!

Part II

MY LESSONS

Chapter 5

Where I Am Today

I have been privileged to go through experiences that enrich my life day after day. I am not unique, nor am I special. I am just like everyone else.

Perhaps you have experienced events that were just as intense or just as difficult as mine, maybe more so. Keep in mind that our lives are not about the events themselves—our lives are about what we do with these events, about how we receive them and use them. Do we use our experiences to evolve our thinking? Or do we let them destroy us?

I'm not sure who I would be today if I had had an easy life. But what I am sure of is that my success and happiness were triggered by my evolution, which resulted from my hardships.

In Part II of this book, I share how my life events brought me to where I am today, what I have learned, and which habits I have acquired to make life pleasurable. I also invite you to practice techniques that will saturate your life with inner peace, gratitude, and love, which will activate your powers. I encourage you to start a journal, since some of these exercises require writing.

A lot of people are fascinated by my journey. But this fascination is often related to my recordable achievements—my academic credentials, status, professional position, and wealth—because, for most of us, these are the benchmarks of happiness.

Indeed, status, position, and money can make our physical lives more comfortable, but happiness is totally disconnected from such elements—at least it is for me. When I look at my whole life, when I take the time to notice and appreciate what's in my life (which I do every day!) and what brings me joy, material possessions and physical achievements are not the first things that come to mind.

When people ask me, "Where are you today?" I answer honestly: *I take very good care of my physical and spiritual selves, and I feel love and gratitude every minute of my life.*

I am always scanning the Universe for guidance, and when I receive it, I reflect on it, learn from it, and act on it. The most pleasurable moments of my life are moments of love—love toward everything and everyone I interact with. Love triggered by contributing to others, by serving others, by activating evolution in others, by sharing with others. Because when we give love, we generate love, and those of us who have experienced living in a total state of love can relate to how powerfully amazing it is!

I'm in a beautiful cycle of constant learning: When I share my experiences and my thoughts, I learn from the response. I learn from the emotions. And the results not only validate my own knowledge but generate more queries and evolve my state of mind. This process keeps me constantly hungry for my truth, for knowledge.

Every day I meet a new *me*, a me who has learned something new or touched someone's heart for the first time, felt the exhilaration of smelling a just-blossomed flower, or realized that my universal power inspired me to make an important decision. Everything that happens, whether it is perceived by people as good or bad, is a lesson or a message—or sometimes a beautiful reward. You see, if there is a new, evolved *you* every day, you will never age! We are designed to get wiser not older; if we feel the pleasure of gaining wisdom, we needn't worry about aging because we'll meet a new version of ourselves every day.

I have been guided to make healthy decisions in my life and to open myself to the lessons of my journey. I work hard to keep my emotions elevated. I do everything I can to protect myself from negative feelings, and I control my ego so it understands it is not my master. I am married to someone who supports my inner peace, and my heart is filled with love and gratitude toward him. I have two boys who have driven my search for the truth and my evolution both emotionally and intellectually. I work with a boss who consistently offers me respect, unconditional support, and trust. I work with a team that inspires me, a team that fills my days with love, dreams, and more love. I am grateful to all of these people.

I am where I need to be—learning, laughing, and loving. These are the three *L*'s of my life. As long as I'm in an environment that nourishes my three *L*'s, I know I'm on track to continue my journey of evolution.

What I've Learned from Life

Some people point out that I've had a hard life, that my story is a sad one. I nod my head. Yes, I've had many difficult moments, and there are even more of them, ones I've chosen not to share in these pages. But then I smile at these kind people showing me concern and empathy, and I say to them, "Where would I be without these difficult moments? I cherish them because they carried me to my beautiful present." I can't imagine where I would be without the challenges I faced and the tests I passed. What matters is how I used the hard times to produce a wonderful state of being.

You see, what I want to share with you is how to evolve your thinking—to see the good that comes along with what you perceive as the bad, the successes that follow the hardships. Many of us get stuck in negative thinking—whether it is in looking at our own difficult situations or those of someone else—and we tend to see only the ugly, scary stuff. We don't realize that the ugly, scary stuff may be what will get us to where we want to go, either directly or indirectly. Maybe these things are rocks in our path, and because they are scary, we might take a turn to avoid them, leading us to exactly where we need to be.

The good news is that you can just as easily see the good and beautiful things in life. And I promise to show you in the following pages how I did it. I will demonstrate how to shift from feeling victimized to feeling powerful. I will show you that your reality is your own creation and that events—no matter how painful they seem—can be a major force in helping you discover your powers. Moreover, my wish is for you to experience your own lessons, so that you can enjoy your own journey, witness your powers come to life, and discover the joy of helping others and sharing with them.

Here is a list of the key lessons
I've acquired from my life so far:

- **I learned that I am free and magical**, and that the power of the Universe is available to me if I choose to reach out to it.

- **I learned that my most important challenge is to keep my mind clutter-free and clear**, and to not allow negative thoughts to distract me.

- **I learned that I must make an effort to stay connected**, so that I don't forget who I am and, more importantly, that the Universe is here watching over and guiding me.

- **I learned that I am in control**. I choose what to receive and what to reject—and if I choose not to receive negative emotions, they have no way of affecting me.

- **I learned that I decide what to pay attention to**. I determine whether others are allowed to confiscate and control my mind. I can choose to control my own thoughts or to absorb the thoughts and beliefs of others.

- **I learned that fear is an illusion created to control my behavior**. And if I don't acknowledge the fear, it doesn't exist for me.

- **I learned that dreaming is the first step in achieving dreams.**

- **I learned that I have the power to either feed negativity or demolish it**, and I choose to continuously demolish it.

- **I learned that my present is precious** and it is all I have. I feel the present moment and react only to it. Past negative emotions will not cloud my judgment; they only exist if I bring them back to life.

- **I learned that I interpret the meaning of things by using my personal filters**, so I must keep my filters clean and healthy. If I don't do the maintenance work, I may misinterpret situations, leading to poor decisions.

- **I learned that behind every pain is a lesson**, along with the possibility of evolution and relief. I need to focus on the journey, not the event, and feel the excitement of where my journey is taking me instead of drowning in the pain of the event.

- **I learned to make an effort to remember the Universe** and be alert to its messages. If I don't, I run the risk of forgetting that it's there, because I am constantly bombarded with noises trying to focus my attention on the material world.

- **I learned that my most important enemy is my most important asset: my mind.** If I keep it healthy, it will help me see; but if I neglect it, I will become blind.

Chapter 6

Where Are You Today?

What does *happiness* mean to you? I don't ask this as a rhetorical question. I really think it's an important idea to define for yourself. I invite you to pause for a moment and really sit with this question. What are your benchmarks for happiness? Are they class status, job title, and income? How much power you have? The car you drive? The house you live in? Which university your child goes to? The number of countries you have visited? Your assets?

Now I invite you to try the first of several exercises in this section of the book.

▼ ▼ ▼ ▼ ▼ ▼ ▼ ▼ ▼ ▼ ▼ ▼ ▼ ▼

Defining What Happiness Means to You

Please, right now, grab your journal. Turn to a fresh page and list what you believe makes you happy. Consider big and little things, using the examples of the benchmarks above as a start. Make your list as long as it needs to be, including whatever reflects (or would reflect) your happiness, but leave plenty of space between each benchmark to write more later.

Next, note whether you already have the item or if you want it.

Then, ask yourself, *Why do I think the things I listed will make me happy?* Try to drill down to the details to truly understand what will make you happy.

For example, if one of the things on your list is a beautiful house, ask yourself, *Is it the house that will make me happy or enjoying the house with my family?* In other words, if you lose the family and keep the house will you remain happy? You can do this with other items on your list: Is it the car that will make you happy or driving it to your job? If you lose the job will the car continue to make you happy? Does the job make you happy because you love doing the work or because it communicates a certain social status? Will you still enjoy doing the job if you lose the social acknowledgment? Do you want money because you want to increase your net worth and get the respect of your community, or do you want money to use it on truly pleasurable activities or helping others?

Go through every item on your list and ask yourself these important questions. Write down your answers. You owe it to yourself to know what makes you happy so that you can focus your efforts on your happiness. If you don't, you will spend your life working for things you *believe* make you happy, only to achieve them and realize that you made a mistake and you're still unhappy.

How did completing this exercise feel? Did you notice anything? We will build on this exercise shortly, to continue defining what happiness means to you. But for now I want to talk about comfort versus happiness.

Look at your list and circle all of the things that have to do with status, position, power, and money. You might have made a lot of circles, and that's okay. Now consider whether these objects bring you *comfort* or *happiness*. Look at the reasons you listed. Is it possible that they bring you only comfort and not true happiness, and that something else is making you happy?

I differentiate between objects and tools of comfort, and true happiness. It is wonderful to be comfortable; these benchmarks make our lives convenient and easy. But consider that they don't really equate to happiness. Rather, they are objects of power that come with great responsibility. And if you can't acknowledge that these are merely objects and tools of comfort, then you risk becoming their slave by mistakenly linking them with your happiness. Remember that happiness cannot possibly come from material things—comfort does—and there is a big difference between happiness and comfort!

▼ ▼ ▼ ▼ ▼ ▼ ▼ ▼ ▼ ▼ ▼ ▼ ▼ ▼

Exploring the Roots of Your Happiness

Let's do another exercise. Return to your journal and your list of happiness benchmarks. Reread what you wrote and what you circled.

Next, pretend that you are a scientist; you're studying yourself nonjudgmentally and are completely open to the outcome. Your job is to investigate the roots of your benchmarks of happiness. Ask yourself, *Where or from whom did I get the notion that this thing will make me happy?* Take your time looking at each item on your list. Write down some likely sources.

You may be surprised to discover that you learned from watching TV that a certain brand would bring you happiness; or from your mother that giving up a career to raise children would bring you happiness; or from society that having the newest smartphone would make you happy. The odds are, your happiness parameters stem from programming in your subconscious. Maybe a memory of when you were growing up drove you to link certain things with happiness. Or perhaps it was subliminal advertising.

In fact, the whole advertising industry is based on this concept. Remember the ads that linked cigarettes with enjoyable friendships? Maybe a lot of what we believe makes us happy is nothing but a successful media campaign or a set of standards engraved in our minds when we were children. Our minds become enslaved by these messages, to the extent that we no longer recognize what comes from our own thoughts versus what comes from external messages that program our thinking.

So my next question is: Are *you* defining your own happiness? Or are you living by the happiness standards of *someone else*?

You see, much of what we think we need to be happy is based on what others and society in general acknowledge as parameters for happiness. We are brainwashed into thinking that money secures happiness, when this notion is far from the truth.

My advice is: Don't follow the money; let the money follow you. Don't make financial success a central objective in your life, because if you do, you may be blinded by it and not see the true opportunities that could lead you to the happiness you are seeking. Start by defining the emotions you want to experience, and from there you will be guided to the career (or partner) that matches these emotions.

More importantly, recognize that you cannot sustain anything you do without passion. If you take a job that you dislike because it pays good money, the odds are your output will be average and you will eventually leave it. Money alone simply cannot sustain happiness! On the other hand, if you are in love with your job, you will succeed; you'll eventually make more money because you are doing it with passion, and this will differentiate you from everyone else—and the money always follows stars.

Is It About Happiness?

Remember how I wrote that I want to challenge you to evolve your thinking? Well, this next exercise is designed to help you clarify the meaning of happiness. Grab your journal and let's begin.

The Happiness Price

Review your list from the previous exercises. Now write down the actual sensation that you wish to experience from each benchmark without using the word "happiness." For example, if a house is on your list, consider what other emotion besides happiness you would feel living in it. Maybe it's "feeling safe" or "feeling appreciated for being recognized by my family as an achiever" or "feeling relieved to have more space to play with my children."

Next, look at your answers and describe the price you would pay to have each item on your list. I'm not talking about money here but rather what you would need to give up. For example, if a bigger house will bring you happiness because there will be more space for your children to play, but you will be working long hours to afford the house, the price you pay is time away from home at work. Ask yourself whether you will have the time to play with your children given the long hours at work, and if yes, whether those moments will be quality time or overshadowed by exhaustion.

Reflect on your answers. Sticking to my example, do you think that your happiness is really tied to having the bigger house? Will your life be sad or dreary without the bigger house? Maybe you decide that playing with your children in a smaller house will actually achieve your desired emotion?

I invite you to consider that "happiness" is an illusion—and that our preconceived notions of what happiness is can be the result of many positive sensations and emotions. In other words, is it possible that we're looking for something that doesn't exist on its own and is only the result of many other positive emotions combined?

Is our relentless drive for happiness a trap that keeps us running in circles, because we are brainwashed into believing that it is achieved through material things? And because it is defined by social norms and materialistic parameters—rather than by what's deep within ourselves, in our state of mind—when we achieve those parameters we don't always feel happy. So, we keep running in the same circle, chasing happiness.

When we feel love, don't we feel happy? When we feel gratitude, don't we feel happy? When we are learning, don't we feel happy? When we help someone, don't we feel happy?

Maybe we need to break free from the illusions created around the term *happiness*. Maybe we need to detox our minds around the definition of happiness. Maybe we need to recognize that achieving a state of happiness is and will remain free of any financial transactions!

In other words, if you gave up *striving* for happiness, my guess is you'd find your way around to it eventually through many other wonderful emotions. That's because striving for happiness, especially when that happiness is defined by someone or something else, is what causes us heartache and headache. That's why we see people spending years of their lives working to acquire or achieve something that they think will bring them happiness, only to realize that, when they have it, it's not making them happy.

I'm not asking you to give up happiness. No way! I'm simply asking you to really understand what it means to you. Just be open to the idea that happiness can be achieved through many other positive emotions and behaviors, that it's not a stand-alone objective—in spite of what you've been taught or have absorbed through other sources.

You Don't Need to Suffer Anymore

Sometimes people ask me, "What did it feel like to go through what you did?" I tell them that it was like being lost in a thick, dark forest that you can't find your way out of. Yet, there was always the excitement of searching for the unknown and trying to achieve my dreams, and I had a deep confidence that walking through the scary woods would eventually get me to my destination safely. I trusted the Universe so much that I surrendered to its power. I trusted that it was always guiding me toward my evolution.

Yes, there were times when I suffered, and yes, there were times when I was frustrated because I wanted things to happen faster, and yes, there were times when I felt lost, anxious, and scared. But I never allowed such negative feelings to dominate my mind for too long. I saw them as red flags of danger, and I always brought myself back to a state of surrender, a state of total confidence that I was not alone and I was being guided toward beautiful, elevated emotions. It was a matter of focusing my attention on the Universe and, despite the exhaustion of going through difficult experiences one after the other, protecting myself from my own fears and anxieties. The Universe always delivered, and my confidence increased with every experience.

But just because I suffered does not mean you have to! Because if I knew then what I know now—if I had had the tools that I am sharing with you in this book—I would have used them to speed up and facilitate my journey.

I've become passionate about sharing what I've learned with people, specifically with those I love, and particularly with my kids. My hope in sharing my life and lessons is that my children and others will be able to see the path guided by the Universe without overburdening themselves with worry and restlessness. My focus is on triggering positivity and joy. I want to see less suffering and more happiness, because there really is no need to suffer. I want to witness people discovering their abilities and activating their natural powers.

In these next pages, I will ask you to make your own decisions about your own life. I invite you to define what it means to you to *live a full life*. The question of where you want to be is crucial. I invite you to clear your mind so that you can hear the universal guidance; it's free and it's here for everyone who chooses to reach out to it.

Chapter 7

The Powers Around Us

We do not live in a bubble. In fact, we are all connected. Every one of us is connected to the others by something magical that I call *universal power*. Whether you call it "God" or the "Universe" is unimportant—let's just agree that it's there. I believe that if people begin connecting to this universal power, they will gain clarity that'll enable them to manage their lives better, suffer less, and discover the treasures of life.

My life experiences, coupled with my research, taught me a great deal about people, about the Universe, about the magical energy that connects everything. I've also discovered how we can adopt certain principles that activate our abilities to connect to this energy, feed on it, and change our circumstances so we can achieve our dreams.

To me there are four major powers that influence the quality of our lives. Some can weaken us; some can empower us. I will discuss each one separately, given their importance:

- The power of society
- The power of learning
- The power of fear
- Our inner powers

The Power of Society

The connection between people and their society is powerful. It drives behavior because society has tremendous influence on our preferences, feelings, values, and behaviors (Fehr & Hoff, 2011). There is a whole social science that talks about human needs, including the need to belong to social groups for our very survival.

Unfortunately, many people have surrendered their belief system and their mind to social norms, so much so that social pressure drives what they do and how they live; it affects their preferences, their values, and their perceptions; all of which determine how they behave and how they choose to live their lives (Gomes, 2011). Social pressure can be so intense that we end up suppressing our emotions to please society, and sometimes we hurt our loved ones by pushing them to conform too.

▼▼▼▼▼▼▼▼▼▼▼▼▼▼

What Are Your Social Pressures?

Grab your journal for another writing exercise. This time, look around you to find evidence of social pressure. Write down what you notice. For example, do you know parents who have decided what their kids will study because it will lead to a career that will ensure social respect? Do you know adults who subject themselves and their families to stringent rules because they worry about social judgment? Maybe you know people who discipline their kids at a young age to teach them conformity. Perhaps you know teenagers who have to resort to rebelling because they want to think freely.

Also write down examples of social pressures you feel. Maybe you struggled to be accepted at school and got bullied because you were different. Maybe you have experienced racism. Or perhaps you were (or are) a talented kid who was deprived of expressing your talents because society didn't value your skills?

When you are done, look over what you have written and notice any patterns or things that surprise you.

Most of us have suffered as a result of social rules. We have been taught that it is in our best interest to adapt to these rules. We have been told to conform to them, and sometimes we put so much energy into adaptation that we become unhappy, depressed, and/or ill. Our preferences are controlled by society. Our choices are driven by society. What is perceived as right and wrong is dictated by society (Fehr & Hoff, 2011).

Societal norms are the reason my father perceived women the way he did, the reason he never enjoyed loving his children, especially the girls. Social pressure drove his every decision. My father was so preoccupied with conforming to social rules that he wasted his life ensuring social acceptance—but at what price? Perhaps it was at the price of our quality of life as a family and at the price of losing closeness with his daughters. Was it worth it?

Ask yourself: *Does conforming to social norms get me a step closer to feeling elevated emotions?* For example, are you a parent who wants your child—regardless of their passions—to become a doctor or an engineer because this earns respect from society?

Every society has its own set of rules, and breaking free of them could yield severe repercussions, depending on the culture. For instance, marrying someone from a different religion could lead to dishonor, excommunication, or even death in some cultures. The questions you need to ask yourself are: *What am I willing to sacrifice for social acceptance? And what is the price of conformity?* For my father, it was losing the close relationship with his daughters.

Is society measuring your happiness or are you your own ruler? Are you able to create balance, to focus on what makes you happy while setting social boundaries?

In general, how much time do we, as people, spend conforming to the pressures of our community versus freeing our minds and activating our dreams? Which is safer: for adults to vigorously prohibit or limit teenagers, which can provoke them to rebel against the suffocation of conformity, or for adults to respect them and allow them to dream? A relationship that keeps them safe by guiding and inspiring them, or a relationship that controls them by prohibiting them?

Understanding my father was important to me, because he was

instrumental in the difficulties of my life. Coming to terms with the enormous role that social pressure played in determining my father's actions was essential to my understanding him. Social conformity was the main driver of my father's actions. Being socially respected was so important to him that he felt he had no other choice but to try to control my life.

We impose discipline because we are afraid that people might do something "wrong" if we don't. But what if people don't need so many rules because they have an inherent sense of what's good and bad? How about taking the risk that people don't need to be disciplined to do the right thing? How about reflecting on the notion that they will probably do the right thing because of love, not because of discipline? Have you ever thought that rebellion might be a result of suppression? Ask yourself: *Why do I impose what I am imposing? Is it because I think this is the right thing to do, or is it because I know that society does not accept the behavior?*

If we agree that connecting to the Universe will enable us to see its guidance and activate our powers, how about we teach our children how to connect? How about recognizing that we don't have the answers, but trusting that when we connect to the Universe we will know what to do? How about recognizing that suppression, prohibition, and stringent rule-enforcing increase stress levels, promote anxiety, and eventually diminish the ability to connect? Maybe we need to recognize that, by imposing our personal will and placing so much pressure on our children, we are deactivating their true powers and throwing them into a state of fear and anxiety—effectively putting them in survival mode.

If you are a parent, you might be training your kids to become hard workers, training them to be ethical. But have you ever considered that maybe you don't need to train them at all—that you simply need to show them? Maybe as your kids watch your behavior, they will learn how to behave? Have you ever considered that core values are not taught, they are lived?

Yes, I am talking about parenting here, because this is where it all starts: We either fuel our kids with anxiety and suppression, or we teach them to think freely. Whatever they learn from us they will carry with them and contribute to their surroundings.

My father was a victim of society, and in turn, because of social pressure, he victimized his family. He was a model conformist, and his mission was ensuring his family conformed too. But when we lived in Canada and had to adapt to a different social system that clashed with his core beliefs, my father began to unravel. He was terrified that his family might integrate into the Canadian environment and break his social values. He had rules to abide by and rules to enforce—in a place that was blind to them. The greater tragedy is that my father died before releasing himself of these societal pressures, before allowing himself to express the love that I am sure he felt toward his children.

Social pressure entraps most of us—in some cultures more intensely than others. There is pressure to conform to gender roles, pressure to have an "acceptable" identity, pressure to believe in one god, pressure to think like everyone else. It's unnecessary and a waste of pure energy, which can be invested in higher-quality relationships. We all experience the discomfort of social pressure.

We must talk about it, so we can collectively free ourselves from it.

When we understand social influence, we understand why people do what they do. When I understood why my father behaved the way he did, it changed my perception of things; instead of looking at my dad as someone who deprived me of an education, as someone who imposed painful conditions on me, I see someone completely focused on being accepted by his society. I realize that he felt so much pressure to keep his reputation intact that he wasn't thinking about my feelings or anyone else's.

Social pressure consumes people. We end up hurting those we love. We believe we're protecting them from themselves, but we restrain them to protect our own reputation and ego. We are so desperate to be accepted by our social groups that we start living for this purpose. This need to be accepted by society drives our decisions—how we live, how we dress, how we raise our children. We get stuck in a vicious cycle: reacting to the noises of society instead of nurturing our own thoughts.

As time goes by, we tire of conforming, and we realize that we have let too many years go by without enjoying the real pleasures of life—starting with loving our family members. I keep thinking that my dad left this world before giving me a real hug. What a shame! I know that my father was filled with loving emotions toward us, but he was so busy striving to maintain a good reputation and social approval that he never had the time to enjoy his love.

Society's Bias Toward Our Physical Selves

Another aspect of modern society that limits our growth is an emphasis on our physical self—that is, our physical body—which is separate from our spiritual body. We are consumed by the physicality of our existence. This is no surprise, because we are bombarded with messages from advertising, the Internet, and other forms of communication that tell us what is favorable and what is not in terms of physical appearance. We're told what to buy, where to visit, what job to have. And because most of us would like to fit in and feel as if we belong to our community, we tend to pay attention to these messages. It's easy to model our lives on and talk about what we can see and physically touch.

You may be wondering, *What's the problem with that? It doesn't seem bad to me.* The problem isn't with these things themselves. The problem lies in the fact that our society's overwhelming focus on "physicality" doesn't leave space for the other facets of our lives.

We work like robots. We have no time to enjoy the basic pleasures of life. We exhaust ourselves trying to achieve status. We are coerced into poor relationships. We are governed by rules to conform. We labor to earn money to live comfortably. And we spend our lives searching for happiness. Take a look around you: can you identify the material things that are enslaving you to societal ideals?

▼▼▼▼▼▼▼▼▼▼▼▼▼

Explore Your Priorities

Take a few minutes to think about what you would do with $10,000. What would you prioritize spending the money on? Write this down in your journal.

Next, reflect on each item you listed and describe why it is a priority.

When you are done listing your reasons, read what you wrote. Do you see any patterns? Perhaps you notice that some of your answers are influenced by external messages and are not necessarily your own priorities. For example, you may have written that a smartphone is your priority, and your reason is that everyone has one. Ask yourself, *Is this my own priority? Or did it become my priority because of societal pressure?* If your priority is prompted by societal pressure, consider whether you are enslaved by social norms that promote physical possessions.

We are bombarded with messages focusing our awareness towards our physical state; the majority of these messages are trying to persuade us to purchase something. They're creating the need for whatever material things they are selling.

Let's take a simple example: How many times a day do you

notice advertising that involves making our bodies look perfect? Consider ads you see on TV, social media, billboards, and various websites for the perfect diet, the best exercise routine, healthy eating habits, weight loss, or appearance.

We are all guilty of being lured in by the promise of an "ideal" body. And so, in our striving for "perfection," we aren't authentic and may wind up hurting ourselves. Many of us end up overeating, emotionally eating, or starving ourselves as a result of psychological issues brought on by this pressure (from advertisers, society, peers, and even our own families) to conform to an ideal!

This bias toward the physical dimension of our life means we don't spend time on the other dimensions. But we are not just physical bodies, after all. As we are encouraged to eat well and exercise, we must do the same for our emotional, psychological, and spiritual dimensions. Wouldn't it be nice if this were the social norm?

Remember, if we conform to one aspect of society, there will be another and another. . . . And we may become stuck in a cycle that drains our energy to gain social acceptance and achieve financial success. We must wake up and break this cycle.

It's time we take things into our own hands. It's time we recognize that we are part of the social conformity problem, and that conformity often turns its participants into victims at some point in their lives. It's time to acknowledge that rebellion and risky coping behaviors may be the results of this pressure to conform.

It's time to calm our minds, have some silence, connect with our Universe, and fill our hearts with love and gratitude so we can change our world and contribute to others that may need our support.

Let's free ourselves, so we can free society. Let's break the controlling systems and invest in human potential. Let's unleash the power of individuals and watch them create a better reality. Let's not create victims anymore; let's support human potential. It's time to trust that removing extreme societal pressure is more likely to lead to people living in harmony—because harmony cannot be forced.

Let's release the fears that drive us to try and control everything. Let's be brave and trust in the universal power. Let's encourage collaboration and sharing of thoughts. Let's create a society that is driven by love instead of power and fear. We make up our society and we control how we want to live, so let's use social influence to support and encourage people to grow and evolve.

The Power of Learning

Learning is one of our basic, core human functions, so we cannot neglect it (Kolb, 1983). If we are not learning, we are triggering the cycle of aging and death. Learning is the door to freedom. The learning I'm talking about is not about memorizing data—it's about nurturing our ability to continuously receive and take in information. Learning, to me, is a state of mind; it is not an activity that one does at specific times of day (Marquardt, 1999). You see, in a dynamic environment like ours, the focused technical learning that we know today will be irrelevant tomorrow. So, true learning is about our ability to constantly digest new information and integrate it into our life. It's about being connected to information and about how "fit" we are to capture the meaning of what is happening around us.

Learning remains a fundamental element in my life. In fact, it was what drove both my spiritual evolution and my general life evolution. Learning powered my resilience and enhanced my life with excitement for a brighter future. Without learning, I would still be the sad typist who sees herself as a victim. Without learning, I would have been a slave.

Connect Your Mind

For true learning to happen, it's important to recognize and practice a few fundamentals:

- Develop a readiness to learn.
- Cultivate a hunger to learn.
- Recognize that learning is a lifestyle, not an activity.
- Reflect back on what you have learned.

Think of it this way: If your phone is not connected to Wi-Fi, it can't download any information. It works the same with humans. If you are not connected and ready to receive information, you will not learn much—or at least you will not receive the information you need to make good decisions. If you are not ready to receive, your mind will be cluttered with information fabricated to brainwash you and bombarded with messages that aim to control you.

Therefore, it's important that we develop and value a readiness to learn. When we are ready to "download" information intuitively at any time, we are living in inquiry mode (Marshall, 1999), which means we're constantly searching to understand, to receive, and to connect with events and situations. This learning process is a state of mind that will direct you toward the information you need to ultimately drive your evolution.

It's also important to know that you were designed to connect and receive information—it's a natural ability that you have. You have inherent wisdom. You have intuition. Regrettably, we have shifted our attention away from this power and focused instead on receiving and conforming to external social messages—so we are not "exercising" this ability to connect. All we need to do is remember to practice. All it takes is deciding that this functionality is important to you and understanding that you need to activate it. It takes some effort, but it's a different kind of effort than, say, cramming in information for a test. As you practice simply learning to connect and receive, your learning muscles will grow stronger, and learning will become as easy as breathing!

When I think back to major milestones in my life, I can see that my inspiration to act was always triggered by my "receiver" constantly scanning the world around me to find opportunities to improve my life. I didn't really know at the time that I was opening myself to learning, but that's exactly what I was doing—connecting, being ready to receive, and having a hunger for information.

So how did I receive? No matter how sad I felt, I always found time to calm my mind. With a calm mind, I was able to ask for guidance, to search for messages, and to dream of a better future. My challenges did not lie in the complexity of the problems but rather in the difficulty of calming my mind.

Let me give you some examples. Had I become angry at my father for not allowing me to attend a university, I would have probably spent most of my life angry, and this anger would have fueled my reactions; I would have been focused on vengeance, or showing him how furious I was, or doing something purposefully to dishonor him. But what would I have achieved? I would have secured a miserable life and, while being blinded by anger, would not have seen the opportunities presented to me. My life would have been a big waste of time!

Instead, and despite the fact that I was sad, I immediately started searching for something positive in my new situation; I had always believed that in every difficult situation there is a great opportunity. I started looking for the messages. How did I do that? Well, I never stopped dreaming. But not only did I dream, I *lived* the dream: I visualized the pleasure of living out my fantasy and feeling the gratitude for fulfilling my wish.

Remember when I dreamed of Ghassan? I would take time every night to close my eyes, disconnect from reality, and imagine being with him. I would feel the joy of living with him, I would feel being in the garden with him, and I would experience the emotions as if they were real. And because I felt them, they were *real*. I felt gratitude every time I dreamed, and the more I dreamed, the more gratitude I felt and the happier I became. Yes, I eventually woke up to a sad, lonely reality. But no matter how difficult my reality was, I always made time to dream—and the pleasure of my dreams was always more powerful than the hardship of my reality! I allowed myself to experience a range of emotions. That was a powerful gift—to receive love and happiness anytime, anywhere—that no one could take away from me.

When I accepted that I wouldn't have the chance to go to university at seventeen and that I would be working instead, I started visualizing becoming successful. And in those dreams, I was grateful for my success. Just a few years later, at twenty-one years of age, I was a senior manager—not bad!

My dreams inspired me to think and do things outside the box. I found myself challenging everything and continuously searching for solutions. I was always in receiving mode. This enabled me to perform at such a high level. I focused all my energy on performing to compensate for my lack of education. As I dreamed, I optimized the efficiency of my "receptors," and I assure you that every success in my life was guided by an information download as I dreamed of a better future.

Here is what I am trying to tell you: No matter how difficult your circumstances are, you have the power to break free. The power lies in your thoughts and in your heart. The only thing that can turn you into a victim is if you give your circumstances power over your mind and heart.

Remember that your ultimate weapon is your ability to connect, learn, and reflect. If you protect this ability, you will always achieve your desires, despite any obstacles or pain you might face.

Are you ready to find this ability within you? You will learn how to do this in the chapter "One Core Step: Connect, Trust, Accept."

Barriers to Learning

Having an open mind can be hard. Why? Because we are groomed to be *biased* based on cultural norms. For example, in some cultures, we are expected to socialize with only people from a certain religion, which can then hinder us from keeping an open mind about people from other religions. Other cultures impose other restrictions; wherever you go, there are biases thrown your way, biases that you need to be able to see clearly so you can manage them and not allow them to affect your thinking.

The hard part to being open-minded is deciding to open your mind in the first place. You must decide to be open—and you must decide again and again, until it becomes a personal characteristic. Be willing, and with practice your receptors will remain open.

Another obstacle to learning and connecting is our own *negative emotions*. There are two feelings that you need to protect yourself from: fear and anger. Consider them as two of the most dangerous viruses a person can be exposed to.

When you allow fear and anger to drive your behavior, you have surrendered your powers to the people or things you fear and hate. Think about that for a moment. Do you really want to do that? If you're consumed with fear and anger, your mind will constantly be analyzing how to defend yourself, how to confront the situation, or how to run away from the situation. All three are natural defense mechanisms that are meant to protect us from temporary dangers at limited times in our lives. They are *not* intended to be used constantly in our day-to-day lives, because we will become exhausted and eventually get sick.

That said, there is some good that can come out of fear—if we harness it and learn from it. We'll learn all about fear in the next section. For now, keeping your thoughts healthy and free from anger and fear pollutants will strengthen your receiving abilities, which yields to learning. Once you're learning, there is nothing you cannot do. You will be able to use your intuitive abilities to make decisions that will ensure the life you want.

The Power of Fear

Fear's most basic function is to drive us toward safety during times of real danger. Being afraid of dangerous situations is an essential evolutionary trait—it ensures our survival. The risky thing about fear, though, is the length of time we experience it. We were not designed to live in constant fear, because being in survival mode all the time is not sustainable (Dispenza, 2012). To live in a state of constant fear is simply not living. And the moments when we feel fear are moments when we cannot grow, dream, or create.

Research has shown that there are three main reactions linked with fear: confronting, running, and hiding. These are normal and appropriate responses to real danger, such as a legitimate threat to our lives. But sometimes we confront, run, or hide when we aren't in any real danger, which is harmful to our health. We certainly don't want to be reacting this way to perceived threats over long periods of time (Dispenza, 2012).

When fear is triggered in the absence of real danger, it nevertheless communicates to our brain that the threat is real. Our brain treats the false information as truth, creating the illusion that we are in danger. In turn, our mind sounds the alarm to fight, run, or hide so we can protect ourselves. This fear response is linked to many chronic problems, including stress, personal insecurities, and severe illnesses.

Think about it. Have you ever been so stressed about a school or work project that you couldn't do the work? Or felt so insecure about a meeting that you lost your train of thought? Or were so worried after hearing news about an earthquake that you sat in fear waiting for it to happen? Have you ever acted based on fear, only to later realize that it was in your head and nothing happened to actually justify your fear?

If I analyzed every failure of my life, I could link it to a time when I was afraid. As I think back, anytime that I had been afraid I had also felt crippled; I could not dream of anything, could not see anything positive in my situation. I felt like a victim. Sometimes I was so afraid and anxious that my whole body, not just my mind, would collapse; I would lose all my potential, my abilities, my strength.

▼ ▼ ▼ ▼ ▼ ▼ ▼ ▼ ▼ ▼ ▼ ▼ ▼ ▼

Write a Fears List

Think of times when you were afraid. If it is not too triggering for you, grab a journal and write about moments when you were fearful—maybe a time when your company was automating tasks and you feared losing your job, or when you worried about being fired because a colleague close to your boss was spreading rumors about you, or when someone you loved was ill and you were anxious about their condition, or when you worried about making ends meet because your partner lost their job.

Think of what you did to deal with your fears. Describe how you handled (or didn't handle) the situation.

Next, describe all the things that you could have done to reduce your anxiety. For example, you could have gotten excited about the automation so that you could be equipped to do a different, more-fulfilling job. Or you could have calmed your mind so that you stayed poised when you met with your boss, who would then realize that what they'd heard about you could not be true (isn't that what happened to me?). Or you could have stayed positive and surrounded your loved one with positive energy to help them to heal. Think about how the situation could have been more enjoyable had you not allowed fear to saturate you.

When you are done writing, reflect on the effects of fear. How does it keep us stuck and unable to shift into a positive state of mind that would empower our thoughts and actions?

A lot of times, we can do very little about such situations, but we build a worst-case scenario in our mind and we start living it. And the more we live it, the more fearful we become. The key is to calm our mind, connect to the Universe, and decide how to react when we actually see the reality unfold in front of us.

Another important thing to acknowledge is that fear has been used as a tool for centuries to control behavior by neutralizing our powers (Baker, 2009). Fear deactivates our basic natural functionalities: instead of dreaming we worry, instead of creating we stress, instead of sharing we protect our ideas (Lipton, 2016). Fear drives us to constantly analyze the details of our circumstances and to be on high alert about how to stay safe. Fear prevents us from calming our minds and receiving the inspiration that the Universe has waiting for us.

Let me give you another example. When I was working at the investigation company and my boss was harassing me, I was very bothered and very uncomfortable. But instead of being afraid that I would be fired for not accommodating him, I focused my attention on my work and ignored his behavior. My commitment to my job was witnessed by the owner, which led to me being free of the manager's bad behavior. Now, what do you think would have happened if I had been afraid of losing my job? I would have probably accommodated the manager, and how do you think things would have turned out? I assure you that my attention would not have been on my work, and I would not have gotten promoted. Who knows where I would be right now?

The moment I understood that fear could be used to control my mind, I decided that I would not let that happen to me. My mind is too precious to hand over to someone else. I would not be someone's scared puppet. Over time, I began to teach myself to be aware of when I was starting to feel scared. I would focus my attention on the positive outcomes of my dreams instead of thinking of the worst outcomes. Researcher and scientist Joe Dispenza (2012), in his book *Breaking the Habit of Being Yourself*, states that "where you place your attention, you place your energy." What value would I get out of placing my attention on something that worries me?

My father was so terrified of being judged by society that he spent his whole life defending his turf and controlling his kids. He made sure that none of us did anything to make society reject him. My father's fear devastated him—and he's not alone! Most of us live with fear every day of our lives; it's such a familiar feeling that we perceive it as normal.

Whether we have good intentions or bad, the fact is that we use fear to control the behavior of others. As a result, many people end up living in defense mode; instead of growing we become exhausted. This needs to stop. Living in fear means we're missing out on living; we're missing out on loving. We're missing out on creating, and we're forgetting how powerful and magical we are.

We must break free. We must understand that fear controls us and love frees us. We must take control of our emotions and our lives, and create societies based on acceptance, tolerance, and harmony. We must recognize that diversity enables learning. When we stop learning, we start dying!

Our Inner Powers

When I looked back on my life to understand how I overcame my hardships, I realized that throughout the most difficult times of my life, one thing I did consistently was reach out to the Universe and tap into its power. I didn't know that was what I was doing, but in hindsight, praying, talking to God, and clearing my mind were my ways of connecting my mind to the Universe's Wi-Fi network.

No matter how sad my life seemed at the time, these moments of connection always resulted in something great happening: a new opportunity, a new possibility, a fraction of a dream materializing, or the start of a new dream. Remember the office manager who was harassing me? I ignored him, didn't focus on fearing job loss, and prayed. I asked for God's help, for guidance and protection. The end result was acknowledgment of my commitment to work and total freedom from the ugly situation I had been in.

But how was I doing this? I seemed to do it naturally, without thinking. If I could comprehend how this relationship with the Universe worked, I could begin to do it consciously, and I could share it with others. I needed to understand why I experienced surges of power during the most difficult of times, power that always pulled me from suffering to peace, from hopelessness to hopefulness. Was this only about me? Was I special? Did I have special powers? How exactly was I creating my desired reality?

As I tried to answer these questions, I reflected on how I felt as I was facing events in my life. I thought about what I did and what I did not do, and I tried to deduce the main abilities that I used. As I reviewed the events of my life, I began to understand an important lesson: I was not special.

I am just like every other person. And every other person is just like me. Every person has a power within himself or herself to overcome hardships and reach for their dreams. All of us! The key to my success and achieving my dreams, I learned, was my mental state of mind and my attitude.

And so, if you are struggling, know that you may need to look at your state of mind and attitude, which you can change to live a healthy, thriving life.

The Power of Our Thoughts and Emotions

Dr. Joe Dispenza, in his book *Breaking the Habit of Being Yourself*, said that our subconscious is responsible for 95 percent of our habits and behavior. So we need to pay attention to our thoughts and take control of our mind in order to remain the master of our behavior.

Emotions trigger a certain pattern of thinking. For example, if we are angry at someone, we start thinking about vengeance; which triggers more anger, because we start living and reliving the experience, which intensifies our emotions and exaggerates them. The same way dreaming of a beautiful experience gives us joy, as if we are actually living the experience, visualizing a negative experience causes us to feel the negative emotions and thoughts of that situation. We start imagining the scenario of vengeance in detail, and the more details we add, the more anger we feel—and the cycle goes on.

Although the greatest danger of this cycle plays out if we allow ourselves to move from visualization to implementation, the fact remains that living the vengeance in our minds is detrimental to our health and our state of mind. It's critical that we stop our thoughts and turn them around so that we don't create a negative reality and get stuck in it.

I've watched people become overpowered and controlled by their negative thoughts, ultimately being demolished by them. As I benchmarked my experiences and my emotions against others', especially situations when people were drowning in their sadness and felt victimized, I realized that such negative situations are driven by our surrendering our power to negative emotions and becoming enslaved to anger, fear, and hate. In my case, the times when I felt overpowered by destructive emotions were short-lived. They were brief because I would see the negative emotions start to creep up on me and immediately turn them off; my mind had learned that they were my enemy, and I was committed to not surrendering to this enemy.

Negative thoughts and emotions are the most dangerous enemies of all, because if you don't notice them, they will take control of your heart and mind. When you learn to notice the negative emotions starting to take over, you can begin to shift your attitude and melt these emotions away. You will learn how to do this in "The Five Guiding Principles" chapter.

The Power of How We Interpret Situations

How we interpret or make sense of information and situations drives how we behave. When we see situations or receive information, we process this input and interpret it based on our own biases, beliefs, and value system. Therefore, understanding the power of our interpretation abilities is key to understanding our reactions and behaviors.

For example, when I was hired by the consulting firm and paid substantially less than my male counterpart, I could have decided that the company was unfair and that I would always be paid less than the men working there. This attitude would have probably led to me becoming unmotivated, which would have destroyed my ability to outperform others at my job.

But instead, I assumed that I was paid less because I had not yet proven myself. I believed that if the company saw how valuable I was, they would increase my compensation as my value increased. This led me to work hard without feeling victimized, which resulted in excellent performance, leading the company to substantially increase my compensation.

In other words, my interpretation of the situation motivated me to work harder and prove myself; if I had chosen a different interpretation, I may have felt victimized and either quit or take an action that would've gotten me fired. Instead, I refused to acknowledge the negative elements of the situation.

Interpretation is crucial, because it is this outlook that drives our behavior toward either staying stuck or transforming. It's critical that we recognize the risks in interpreting things in a negative manner.

Here's another example: One day after taking a spinning class, I was approached by the instructor. She said, "I notice that you look at your watch frequently. Do you find the class dull?"

"No! I don't find it boring at all!" I replied, "The truth is, I always look at my watch to check my heart rate."

Her interpretation was that I was checking the time to see when the class would be over, but that was far from true. We go through situations like this every day, when we make assumptions based on how we interpret what we see. Many times, our interpretations are inaccurate, but nevertheless we act upon them.

How we interpret events is unique for each one of us because we have complex, unique variables that come into play. Our experiences and our pain shape the way we decipher information. This is important to recognize; it allows us to understand the behavior of others and cultivate empathy for them.

For example, I am sensitive to father–daughter relationships, given my history with my dad, so when I see a father hugging his daughter, my interpretation is that he doesn't fear society and that his love for his child is more powerful than society's influence on him. My interpretation stems from my emotional desire to have a good relationship with my own father, whose ability to express his love to me was crushed by his sense of duty to conform to social standards. Someone else witnessing this same father hugging his daughter might interpret the act differently.

Our ability to interpret situations differently leads to creativity. When we are capable of comprehending and leveraging our ability to make sense of things from differing points of view, we can see situations from a wider lens. This makes it easier for us to think outside the box and see opportunities that we might normally overlook in the absence of an expanded viewpoint.

But why do we find this so difficult to do? Why do we try to get people to conform to one interpretation, to one way of doing things? Why are we so concerned with controlling other people's thoughts and behaviors?

We Are in Control

Someone once asked me sarcastically, "Why does God look after you only?" My response was that the Universe has made available to us limitless power, accessible by anyone who wishes to tap into it. It's not about *me*. It's about *us*. It's about the choices *we* make as we deal with difficult situations in life.

The truth is that we all carry the power, but we get distracted by negative situations and negative emotions and forget how to use it. If there is anything we should be focusing on, it's who we are and what we are capable of doing!

In life, we all have choices to make. How we respond to situations will either keep us stuck in the cycle we're in or move us toward our goals, our dreams, and our authentic self. We make choices every day. Before you choose, consider how you're interpreting things and whether you're leaning toward the negative or the positive. Consider the choice that best demonstrates who you want to be in the world, and always keep in mind that negativity will yield negativity, keeping you stuck in a vicious cycle.

Let's look at some of the choices I've had to make in my life:

The first major choice I made was to keep hate and anger out of my heart when dealing with my father and his fears. Hatred and anger would have placed me in a state of turmoil and may have caused me to rebel and try to get even with my dad. Instead, I allowed myself to feel hurt and sadness; these feelings helped me to adapt to temporary situations, be patient, and strengthen myself. I calmed my mind, prayed, accepted, and started looking for opportunities.

The second major choice that defined me was one I made at age seventeen, when I was given the option of exacting revenge on the manager who was harassing me. Instead, I chose gratitude for being recognized as a hard worker, and this changed my future for the better. I truly believe that vengeance would have sent me down a dark path, as it had for the manager, whose own job was ultimately taken from him after his attempt to punish me for ignoring him failed.

Remember when I fired my employee on Christmas Eve? That was the third major milestone in my life. This incident awoke in me a desire to always put people first in my life. I realized that people's feelings are important, and I vowed to serve them to the best of my abilities going forward. Had this experience not awoken my compassion, I would probably still be a manager doing the same things and feeling miserable.

The fourth major event that triggered evolution in my life was the release of my ego when I worked with the consulting company. I could have decided that I was a proven "big shot" and I didn't need to learn anything else. But I realized that my ego was a heavy weight, preventing me from learning. Accepting that I was nothing triggered a new journey—a hunger for knowledge.

The fifth milestone was my decision that I would not allow unfair treatment to provoke negativity within me. When I noticed that I was getting paid half of my male colleague's salary, likely because I was a woman, given that I had more experience than my counterpart, I could have allowed it to make me feel victimized or unmotivated, but I didn't. I decided to ignore the inequity and look ahead. I decided to show my worth, which eventually became clear as I grew to be a well-compensated senior manager in the company.

And finally, my seventh choice was my decision to surrender to the universal power as I faced illness!

▼▼▼▼▼▼▼▼▼▼▼▼▼

Review the Role of Negativity in Your Decision Making

I invite you now to explore events in your life and to notice whether negative emotions have kept you stuck in the past. Or maybe they are currently keeping you stuck. Either way, my wish is for you to understand that freedom is within your control, and it is tightly tied to your own feelings. You may do this exercise in your mind, or grab your journal and begin writing.

First, calm your mind and reflect for a moment. Think of a situation when someone hurt you. It could be a simple incident when someone hurt your feelings, or it could be something more severe—the choice is yours.

Now, recall what went through your mind during the incident. How did you interpret that person's behavior? Did you believe there was ill will? Did your interpretation yield negative emotions? Did your own analysis of the situation exaggerate the circumstances?

Next, recall your behavior. Based on your interpretation of the situation, what did you decide to do? How did it work out? Had your interpretation been different, more positive, how do you think the situation would have worked out? Could you have found any positive angles to explain this person's aggression toward you? Reflect on your answers.

This is such an important thinking process, because you don't control when the external storm ends, but you do control your state of mind as you go through it.

What happens if you stay angry? I'll tell you a story of a girl I met in high school in Lebanon. Her parents were divorced, and her dad remarried and had a child with his new wife. This girl was bitter and angry about the breakup and the second marriage. She hated her new younger brother and the likelihood that she would have to share her inheritance with him. So what did she do? She decided to study law with the sole intent of inheriting her father's law firm. She didn't like being a lawyer, but what she disliked even more was the idea that her brother might inherit it too. Fast-forward thirty years, this woman is a lawyer working at her dad's law firm. And she is still bitter, angry, and unhappy. Her misery is the first thing you see on her face. Nothing changed for her except that now her body has aged. She is trapped in her own negativity.

Do what you need to do to keep your mind free, so that you glow and inspire others!

The Power of Our Connection to the Universe

If we don't acknowledge that our connection to the Universe can be powerful, we will not invest time in learning and comprehending the factors in our lives that prevent us from connection. Notice I didn't write "invest time in learning how to connect," because we already know how to connect—it's a natural ability we all have. We just need to *remember* to connect, and we need to make it a priority in our life.

Remember that we are not just a physical body, we are also spiritual. We have thoughts and emotions that drive our spirituality, and we have the tools to activate all dimensions. A body without spirituality is a dead body. What do I mean by *spirituality*? It is "the force within human beings thought to give the body life, energy, and power," as defined by the *Merriam-Webster Dictionary*. It is characterized by love, gratitude, peace, forgiveness, and other nonphysical traits, as highlighted by multiple authors including Dr. Jonathan H. Ellerby, in his book *Inspiration Deficit Disorder*. Spirituality is a dimension of awareness (Chopra, 2012). For the purpose of this book, we will refer to the spiritual dimension as the nonphysical dimension, or as the dimensions that also entail our feelings (emotional dimension) and thoughts (psychological dimension).

There are two critical components that we are equipped with to activate our spiritual side: the heart and the mind. Through the heart and the mind, we are able to comprehend and feel everything in our Universe.

Multiple scholars and scientists have made reference to the fact that humanity is connected to some type of energy field, leading us to recognize that all of us are connected, somehow, to a bigger power. Credible scientists who have hinted at this connection include Nikola Tesla, the Serbian American physicist; the famous Albert Einstein; and Erwin Schrödinger, the 1933 Nobel Prize winner in physics.

Scientists who have shed light on different perspectives of human potential are many. Recent scientific evidence has opened a new horizon for all of us, urging us to take a step back and recognize abilities available to us if we connect to our higher power. Dr. Joe Dispenza argues that people's powers lie in their thoughts. He asserts that we are wired in a certain way that drives our behavior but that we can change how we are wired to heal ourselves and gain control over our destiny and our future. In his book *Evolve Your Brain* (2008), Dr. Dispenza shares tools that help people connect to the greater power using their thoughts. He also provides scientific evidence showing the impact of thoughts on human healing experiences—evidence that simply cannot be ignored, as it highlights the potential of humanity beyond any doubt.

Gregg Braden, an American author of consciousness literature, argues that there is a strong connection between people and Earth's magnetic field. In his book *The Divine Matrix* (Braden, 2008), he provides evidence from a series of experiments that link the energy of the universe to our world and to people. He claims that people can tap into this energy to improve their relationships and strengthen their connections to others and to the Universe.

The study titled "Electrophysiological Evidence of Intuition: The Surprising Role of the Heart" (McCraty, Atkinson, & Bradley, 2004) provides scientific understanding of intuition and how the body behaves as it responds to an emotional situation; the study highlights the big role that the heart plays in such emotions. Intuition, and what is referred to as "gut feeling," have been credited with a lot of CEO success stories; despite this fact, we fail to support the development of such characteristics through our social networks and education systems. We simply take our powers for granted—maybe it's time to wake up!

Ervin László, a philosopher of science and a supporter of the theory of quantum consciousness, explains in his book *The Intelligence of the Cosmos: Why Are We Here? New Answers from the Frontiers of Science* that "all things are connected." He argues that it is a perfect world that works in harmony. László believes that there is more to the human mind and to human consciousness than what we physically perceive.

Dr. Deepak Chopra writes about the powers of people. He teaches about human consciousness and offers support to help people discover their abilities and live higher-quality lives by calming their minds and changing their perspectives.

My objective in listing these great thinkers is not to convince you of their beliefs. Rather, I am advocating that you open your mind to new possibilities. I'm endorsing the importance of recognizing that we are not just physical bodies and that we have powers that we aren't using because we're too busy getting angry or being afraid.

Thinking of Yourself Holistically

I believe that we are born with great powers. Imagine a strong light shining outward from a jewel in the center of your heart. This light connects to our mother light, the power of the Universe. Remember the movie *Avatar*? Remember when the main character, Neytiri, connects her hair to a tree and energizes herself? Same concept. At birth we have this emanating, connected light. But as we get older, perhaps in order to protect ourselves from pain and suffering, or perhaps as we cope with social pressures, we begin putting layers over our jewel. With every hard life experience, and with every negative message, a new layer is introduced to cover our jewel.

As time goes by, so many layers cover our light that we can't feel the light anymore and we lose our connection to our power supply, the Universe. At this stage, we find ourselves disconnected and lost; we begin living a weak physical, emotional, psychological, and spiritual experience. Instead of using our light, we focus on surviving the pain. We treat our fear and anxiety with pills instead of searching for the truth—and the more pills we take, the more layers we pile on our jewel. We become numb, forgetful, and lost.

Unfortunately, this way of living—this separation between body and spirit—weakens us and primes us to become slaves to our own thoughts, creating a prison built on fear and negativity. To come out of this rut, we must take care of ourselves holistically—that is, we must take care of our physical and spiritual dimensions. The challenge lies in our ability to remember that we are more than just our physical body. We must remember that we are connected, that our body is a representation of our emotions and our spirituality. It's easy to forget about our spiritual self, because all we see is our physical self.

Take a minute and think about this: When you meet someone for the first time, what do you typically look at? Their physical appearance, right? You likely scan their physical body and develop an opinion based on hair color, height, body shape, or skin tone, right? But are we really seeing everything?

When we meet someone, we judge based on what we see, despite the fact that we can *feel* their energy. Because we don't trust our gut feelings, we simply focus on their physical appearance.

Society is obsessed with the physicality of things, so a lot of our discussions center around the physical: money, standards of beauty, and so forth. These conversations are naturally the easiest to have because they involve what we can see and physically touch; the benchmarks are clear and tangible.

How frequently are you part of discussions about what energy feels like, or what it feels like to receive messages from the Universe or to experience events that can be labeled as "miracles"? The majority of people don't spend a lot of time talking about the spiritual realm for several reasons: It's harder. It requires more effort and more thinking about how the conversation will be received. And we risk being labeled as weak or even crazy. With a lot of our energy consumed in pleasing and accommodating our physical reality, there is little energy left to nurture our emotional, psychological, and spiritual dimensions. Can anyone deny that we have intuitive abilities, learning abilities, and creative abilities? Yet, we typically talk about the achievements or the results that are triggered by these abilities; we rarely talk about nurturing such abilities.

▼▼▼▼▼▼▼▼▼▼▼▼▼

Map Out Your Dimensional Tasks

In this exercise, you will determine how much time you spend in the physical dimension versus the spiritual dimension. You may be surprised by what you discover!

Grab your journal or a sheet of paper. Divide the page into four columns. In column one, write down all the things you do daily. For example, brush your teeth, eat, walk the dog, go to work, exercise, listen to music, pray, sleep. In the second column, list the percentage of the day you spend doing each activity.

Label the third column *Physical Dimension* and the fourth column *Spiritual Dimension*. Then, for each of your daily tasks, place a check mark in either the third or the fourth column to specify whether the activity is linked to your physical body or your spiritual self. For the sake of simplicity, think of the physical dimension as anything we need to physically exist or that we do habitually without too much thought, such as eating lunch or watching TV. Anything that caters to our emotional, psychological, or spiritual health can be categorized as part of the spiritual dimension (e.g., listening to music or laughing with your children). Now, some activities may be considered both physical and spiritual. For example, perhaps you take a morning walk (physical dimension) in a very mindful way (spiritual dimension), noticing the plants around you, paying attention to your breath, feeling every step against the ground, and so forth. In this instance, you can check both columns.

When you have completed your list, it's time to do the math. How much of your day is invested in your physical dimension versus your spiritual one? How do the percentages add up? Reflect on your answers! If you are imbalanced, consider ways to have more equity across both dimensions. The following two chapters offer some options.

I hope you see the opportunities to invest in your whole self, and I hope you recognize that you are not only a physical body. You have a spiritual self as well, and it deserves just as much care as your physical body. We must strive to participate in conversations and activities concerning the nonphysical: It takes courage, strength, and willpower, but we can do it. And when we do, we will feel at home! You will learn how to do this in the chapter "One Core Step: Connect, Trust, Accept."

Not Feeding into Negativity

As I sat back and tried to link my attitudes during different phases of my life with my spiritual state, I discovered a clear pattern. My hardships went like this: From within the darkness I would receive a hard smack on the face, and as I was falling down, I would feel disappointment, hurt, anger, and sometimes hate. But these emotions never lasted. The moment I hit the ground, I would accept my reality, ask for help, and search for a bright light, a positive opportunity. Difficult situations would eventually turn into amazing opportunities that would push me to an evolved state. This reoccurring pattern in my life was evidence of how the Universe works.

That is how the pattern of overcoming negativity played out in my life, and it's how it can play out for you. You don't have to stay in the free fall of sadness and anger for months or years; you can make a different choice even before hitting the ground!

For me, two noticeable characteristics dominated my mind once I hit the ground: *acceptance* and *gratitude*. These were the magical keys that would open the door for the light to appear.

Acceptance—of what I can't control and of the Universe taking care of the rest—became my secret weapon and impacted my behavior. To some people, I was too peaceful, too kind. Although being kind is a virtue, for me it wasn't about that; it was about knowing that my anger and negative reactions would keep me imprisoned in my own mind. I sensed that they would diminish my ability to see the potential and move forward. So I had to accept the difficult situation and not feed my anger or negative thoughts.

I couldn't control certain situations, but I could control how I responded to them. I had a choice: stay angry and become angrier, or be open to guidance from the Universe and keep dreaming. The faster I accepted my imposed circumstances, the faster I was able to dream of new opportunities. You will learn more about acceptance in the chapter "One Core Step: Connect, Trust, and Accept."

The feeling of gratitude—that I had landed on my feet, found the light, and passed the "test"—gave me a magical drive to find my way forward. We will talk more about gratitude in "The Five Guiding Principles" chapter. For now, I just want to share that acceptance and gratitude consistently nourished me. They were critical success factors in my evolution and in my ability to constantly feel elevated emotions. And they will do the same for you.

If you are experiencing a challenging situation, and you are feeling drowned in negative emotions, the reality is that you may find yourself years later still stuck in the same ugly circumstances—blinded by pain, feeling victimized, and no longer dreaming—simply because you could not see past your negative emotions to your true potential.

Do not waste your life stuck in a prison made of your own illusions! You truly have the power to free yourself from the pain. Your mind can create a different reality for you. You can be free and happy again!

The Magic Is Real

In 2013, I began investigating the effects of spirituality on organizational achievements. I wanted to understand the impact of enabling feelings of spirituality in the workplace. After seven years of research, I completed *Spirituality in the Organization* (Bou-Diab 2020), a thesis containing evidence that enabling feelings of spirituality in the workplace can lead to an increased sense of belonging, which yields better performance for employees and organizations. If such results affect the business environment, where there are boundaries, imagine the implications on the personal level, where you control the boundaries. Imagine what we can do if we can see the Universe from a new perspective!

Our obstacles are there to bring out our strengths. Sometimes we don't realize how strong we are until we face a challenging situation. If we don't see these situations as obstacles, and instead view them as gateways to opportunity, we will find great treasures that lead us to freedom and happiness. You see, we have passion, and once we activate this passion, our lives become magical.

So what is human functionality? It is intuition. It is passion. It is reflective thinking. It is creation. It is innovation. It is collaboration. It is positivity. It is learning!

We spend hours trying to activate an electronic device, such as a phone. Surely, activating our functionality is also worth our time. When we can plug into the universal power, we can shift our lives from stress to calmness, from reaction to reflection, from submergence in our pain to submergence in our potential.

We must start using all dimensions of our existence to seek guidance. We must free ourselves from slavery—slavery to our fears, doubts, and negative thoughts—and regain control of our minds and our emotions. We must search for answers, and we must have faith and trust that the Universe always presents us with the information we need—we just need to stop and hear it!

It's time to resist living a life of total disconnectedness, resist disregarding the power of our thoughts, resist disregarding the power of our emotions. It's time, instead, to strive for a life that activates all the powers of our dimensions!

Chapter 8

One Core Step: Connect, Trust, Accept

Wake up and turn on your signal!

Learning this core step—*connect, trust, and accept*—is absolutely critical. And yes, it is one integrated step, because the three components cannot exist independently. This step was, and remains, the base of my life and has been instrumental to my achievements. If you commit to doing nothing else in this book but this step, you will be well on your way to changing your thinking and realizing your full potential. When you apply the guiding principles listed in the next chapter to your day-to-day life, practicing this core step will become natural, simple, and practically effortless.

The objective of this step is to calm your mind so that it is able to pick up signals, receive guidance, and make helpful decisions that lead you to actions that are in your best interest. You must clear your mind of expectations and train yourself to connect—and the rest will happen naturally. I am not advocating a mystical journey here; my aim is to get you to do the core step. Where you go from here is dependent on what you need and what you are ready for. I see a real danger in embarking on a journey of spirituality with the aim of only having mystical experiences.

Meditations that promise mystical experiences, extraordinary visions, and so on cannot be guaranteed; expecting and not achieving them can set up a person for anxiousness and stress, which is the exact opposite of what we want to achieve. And despite the fact that I believe such mystical things are achievable, I don't believe that they should be an objective. Again, the magic of meditation derives from an individual's state of mind and the degree to which the person practices meditation. I suggest you don't aim for anything more than calming your mind, because that's all you really need to do—the rest will follow effortlessly.

Think of the Universe as a friend you have known since childhood; throughout your experiences with this friend they have always delivered. If you needed support, they supported you. If you needed guidance, they guided you. If you needed love, they loved you. Never once did this friend let you down. You don't doubt this friend because of the track record you have with them, so you trust that they are there, and you trust that you can rely on them. The more history you build with this friend, the stronger your relationship will be. But you must make the effort to connect with this friend so that they stay on top of mind. Remember what they have done for you, and this will help you validate your faith in them.

Every day, I personally connect with my friend, the Universe. And the more I connect, the more I trust, because this power delivers. The more I trust, the more gratitude I feel, and the more gratitude I feel, the more love is sent my way. And the more I receive it, the more I feel gratitude. This is the cycle I am stuck in now—what a beautiful cycle it is!

How to Connect

At first, connecting will take effort; you'll need to develop new habits. But as you build a track record of milestones that validate your decision, you'll trust the power more and more. And the more you experience this relationship, the more it becomes part of your core. With time, it will take less effort to connect—eventually, you will be connected most of the time! Reaching that state brings effortless inner peace and happiness.

It is important not to have expectations as you connect to the Universe; unmanaged expectations can have a reverse effect, causing frustration, disappointment, or added pressure. You are connecting with the Universe to calm your mind, not to ask for anything. When your mind is calm, everything will flow as it should, and what you need will materialize. Notice I wrote "what you need," not "what you want." Sometimes we want things that may not be good for us, so we must trust that the Universe has a much wider view than our limited vision can offer and that what we need will come to us when we need it. Trust that!

I recommend you start a daily practice of connecting. Initiate your morning with connection so its power can sustain you throughout the day. You may find that initially you need to make a lot of effort to keep yourself focused and calm, but with time this habit—and the benefits that follow in its wake—becomes part of you. Eventually you will find yourself evolving to a whole different level in terms of your ability to remain calm and how you deal with your world.

Here are tips for how to connect to the universe:

- **Set aside time to connect every day.** When you wake up in the morning, as you are opening your eyes, feel gratitude for being alive. Before you look at your phone, give yourself some time to relax and think—but not about your problems; they will be waiting for you later. Sit in your bed, or in any comfortable place, and think of the Universe, or whatever you wish to call it (God, the divine, nature; it doesn't matter). Think of your relationship with the Universe and rest your mind.

- **Try to pair connecting with another activity.** If it is challenging to do this right upon waking, try adding it to a complementary activity you do in the morning. For example, if you jog, connect while jogging. If you get up and go straight to the shower, connect when in the shower. If you relax and look out your window, connect while you do that. Connect by focusing on yourself and the power that created you.

- **Focus on calming your mind.** Connection starts with a thought. Don't think of the past or the future; focus on the present moment. Focus on whatever helps you relax, and disconnect your thoughts from the physical dimension. The key here is not to think about day-to-day life. Do not answer the phone or check emails. Give yourself 10 to 30 minutes to think of nothing except the relationship that links you to your creator. Remember how this creator has delivered on multiple occasions of your life.

- **Release expectations.** As you become aware of this power, ask it for help. Ask it for guidance. Ask to be calm. Ask to have the energy to deal with a tough situation. Don't ask for material things: Don't ask to get promoted. Don't ask to get a salary increase. Don't ask for a car. Ask to feel elevated emotions, and ask to have your powers activated; the rest will come naturally.

How to Trust

I say "what you *need* will come to you," not "what you *want* will come to you," for an important reason. You see, we don't have access to the big picture. What we want might not be good for us. Only the power that can see the full picture knows what is good for us and for our evolution, so we must trust it.

When we connect, we need to release our worries and fears to the Universe so it can decide how to help us. I know this sounds difficult, but I want to give you a tip on how to train yourself to do this. Try to remember events in your life when you were saved from something harmful, or situations when you lost something important to you. After a few years passed, you may have realized that those were actually good things that happened.

Think of a time when you were heartbroken over a relationship ending, only to realize in hindsight that it would have been a disaster if you had stayed together. Think of wishes you had that didn't materialize, disappointments that turned out to be among the best things that ever happened to you. Think of the car accidents you were saved from, of decisions that could have been destructive for you. Remembering such events is important because it will strengthen your trust in the Universe. You'll see that there is a force looking out for you that has delivered many times before.

▼ ▼ ▼ ▼ ▼ ▼ ▼ ▼ ▼ ▼ ▼ ▼ ▼ ▼

Validate Your Trust

Let's try another exercise. Recall three times in your life when you wanted something so badly, that you worked so hard for, but you couldn't have it or it didn't work out. If you'd like, write about the three occasions in your journal. What were the circumstances? Why were they significant to you?

Next, reflect on a later event that made you realize that not getting what you wanted turned out to be a positive thing after all. For example, maybe you didn't get a job you really, really wanted. Although you were heartbroken at the time, later you realized that not getting the job forced you to rethink your career choice, move to a town you now love, and start working on exciting projects that make you truly happy.

All of us have experienced situations like this; remembering them is important and strengthens our trust in our relationship with the Universe. We confirm to ourselves why we must accept and trust.

How to Accept

When you trust in the Universe, accepting becomes easy. You come to understand that what you see is not the complete picture, that there are bigger elements that you don't yet know. So you accept working with what you have, with what is presented to you, under the premise that the Universe will do its part.

Have you ever been faced with a situation at work whereby you felt that you weren't getting credit for something you had done? Likely you became anxious and worried about not being recognized for your work. Nevertheless, you were faced with a choice: Stop working and demand to be credited for the completion of the task, or continue performing the task and trust that at the right time you would be rewarded. Most of us want the recognition immediately. But I invite you to consider what would happen if you let go of the need for recognition. What if you could trust in the Universe that the credit for your hard work would come in due time? The anxiety and worry would fade away as you put your trust in the truth unfolding eventually and at the right moment.

One note that is very critical to convey here: Trusting and accepting does not mean getting lazy and waiting for the Universe to do things for you. It means that you do everything in your power within the reality before you, that you do not try to control what you can't control, and that you trust the Universe to participate and help you.

With time and practice, trusting and accepting will integrate into who you are and how you perceive things. This means that you will work hard and do everything to succeed, and you will not worry about what you cannot control. Remember that you don't have a macro view, so you'll have to trust that what happens will be in your best interest.

Chapter 9

The Five Guiding Principles

Changing your lifestyle to take control of your mind and trigger your desired reality is actually quite simple. All that it requires is already within you. You just have to access these traits and nurture them. The same way you need to take care of your body to keep it healthy, you also need to take care of your mind to keep it activated.

The five principles I share with you are simple. They don't require any tools; they don't require money. They are accessible to anyone who chooses to make the effort and take charge of their mind. You really have nothing to lose and everything to gain if you try them:

- Feel gratitude
- Observe
- Nourish your whole self
- Dream
- Release your expectations

These principles have shaped my behavior and who I am. They have been instrumental to my success and, more important, to my peace of mind. These principles are not something you do, like steps toward a goal. Rather, they are characteristic of how you receive information and react to situations. When you incorporate these principles into your life, they keep your mind calm and clear of negative distractions. And you will notice that connecting becomes easier and takes little effort.

I want to invite you to embark on a new lifestyle, one founded on the key, simple principles that changed my life and helped me through my own struggles. These principles guided my evolution so that I could move from anger to gratitude and from hate to love—and they can do the same for you!

Feel Gratitude

Scientific research argues that gratitude is an important milestone in communicating with the Universe. Dr. Joe Dispenza (2012) includes this notion in his teachings and provides scientific evidence of the changes to the brain when someone feels gratitude and does the work of connecting to the Universe. The HeartMath Institute has published data on the effects of feeling gratitude, and synchronizing the heart and the brain, on a person's state of mind.

One way to understand the effects of gratitude is to think about the difference in our feelings when we are grateful versus when we are ungrateful. When we feel gratitude, we feel love, and when we feel love, miracles happen. We find ourselves feeling positive emotions. But if we feel ungrateful, we are likely to feel entitlement. And when we feel entitlement, we might also feel greed, which can be followed by more negative emotions. The power of gratitude, therefore, is interesting to scientists who want to understand how to achieve a powerful state of mind.

Some might argue that we need something important in our life to feel gratitude. But I would counter that there is *always* something to be grateful for. Remembering the little things that we take for granted can help in reviving and emphasizing grateful emotions.

▼ ▼ ▼ ▼ ▼ ▼ ▼ ▼ ▼ ▼ ▼ ▼ ▼

A Habit of Gratitude

I invite you to begin a gratitude practice. Make this a daily habit.

All you have to do is sit with your thoughts (with or without a journal). Think about, or write down, all of the miracles you're living with. Consider the beauty of Earth, the oxygen you breathe, the moments of love you have experienced, the smell of your favorite flower, the pleasure of dreaming. Your list could be as simple as being grateful for being alive. Just take the time to be grateful!

One of the things I am grateful for is the ability to breathe without pain. You might think this is silly, but if you ever had an operation on your chest, you too would appreciate breathing without pain. Another thing I am grateful for is having access to food. Again, this might seem simplistic, but if you've ever felt true hunger, then you would feel grateful for the ability to fill your belly.

Taking things for granted is the invisible problem we all need to see. We assume that having access to food or the ability to breathe freely are basic givens . . . But are they? Let's be grateful for everything we have, big and small, right now.

As you continue your daily practice, investigate new things to be grateful for. No matter how difficult the situation you are in, it could always be worse. Take note of what you have and feel grateful for it, no matter how insignificant it may seem.

Observe

When you can observe what is happening—to you, to others, to things around you—it allows you the space to try to understand, to hear the guidance. Observing enables you to have a calm mind as you deal with events—and a calm mind will help you define your words and actions. It gives you time to think and to assess the results of your actions before you take them.

When you do not have a calm mind in a difficult situation, you're in reactive mode. In reactive move, your response is exaggerated because it is fueled by emotions. You miss out on details that could justify whatever has made you angry. And most of the time, reacting automatically triggers more negative events and actions. And then regret follows, especially if you realize that you may have misinterpreted the situation. Operating in reactive mode puts you at risk.

Being an observer of your own environment means

momentarily pulling yourself out of a situation and trying to see it with detachment. Being in proactive mode gives you time to take in all the pieces of information that may not be clear to you when you're in the habit of reacting. Being an observer helps you see multiple perspectives. It helps you interpret situations more accurately and see how you're affecting others. When you can observe your influence over others, you can make mindful choices: If the effect is positive, enjoy it; if the effect is negative, correct it. Being an observer saves you from regretting anything you might say or do; it highlights your wisdom.

Observing is a powerful approach, especially when you are in an aggressive situation, with an aggressive person, or in a place where you feel victimized or threatened. In these instances, your reactions can enslave you if you lose control of your thoughts and emotions. Taking an observing stance will keep you free and in control of yourself.

Let me explain what I mean: If someone knows how to push your buttons, and you react, you have become their slave. You have given that person the power of triggering your reaction. You are at their mercy. It's as if you are the TV and they have the remote control.

▼▼▼▼▼▼▼▼▼▼▼▼▼

The Power of Observing

Think about a situation in your life when observing instead of reacting would have been a better approach—perhaps a time when someone said or did something that pushed your buttons, and you immediately replied, only to find out that you had misunderstood the situation. What did you feel? Regret maybe? Write about this experience in your journal, or just sit with the memory.

Now imagine that you are in total control of your behavior. No one can push your buttons to get you to do or say anything you will regret. More importantly, no one can get you to show your weaknesses. In this scenario, you are your own master. Guess what? Becoming the observer gives you this power! It gives you control of your thoughts and, more importantly, your actions. Write or think about how the event may have gone differently if you had taken in all the details and slowed your response—if you had observed before responding.

When in negative situations, don't let your emotions drive you. Stay in control of your own wise response. Here is how you can be an effective observer:

- **Try to remember that it's never about you.** Stay in control. In a difficult situation, it's about the person in front of you. This person may be feeling suppressed, agony, pain, confusion, jealousy, greed, or any other negative emotion.

- **Try to feel empathy instead of anger.** Even if this person is trying to push your buttons, sending you negativity, know that you do *not* have to receive it. Do not let anyone's negativity into your heart. That negativity is that person's emotion to keep. Instead, you may choose to recognize that the negativity could be a reflection of that person's pain. Rather than feel angry in response, try to celebrate your own peace and positivity; the empathy will naturally follow.

- **Be proactive instead of reactive.** *Re*active means responding automatically by meeting the other person's level of anger; this reaction harms you and typically creates a bad situation. *Pro*active means responding wisely with a choice in service of harmony, after you have surveyed all the options; this response allows for growth.

Remember, don't let anyone have power over you or your behavior. Keep your power. Do not react. Be the observer.

Nourish Your Whole Self

The same way you nourish your physical body, you must also nourish your emotional, psychological, and spiritual dimensions. Nourishing the body is the easiest, simply because we see our body daily, and seeing something physically keeps it top of mind.

If we stop eating well and exercising, we feel tired, or we might get sick, which means that the physical body has its ways of keeping our attention focused on it. However, if we feel lonely or angry or disconnected, there's no easy blood test that can tell us that we are ill, which makes caring for our other dimensions challenging. Moreover, the emotional, psychological, and spiritual dimensions are not acknowledged by society as being as important as the physical body. This is why traditional Western medicine primarily treats physical symptoms and why we have to look elsewhere to treat the whole body—mind, body, and soul.

Taking the time to cultivate both physical and spiritual dimensions is important. And keep in mind that physical illness can often be the result of emotional, psychological, or even spiritual imbalances. On the flip side, if we are emotionally and psychologically healthy, the odds of being physically healthy are high.

Here are a few simple ways to keep your nonphysical dimensions healthy:

- **Spend time in nature.** Nature is one of our core energy sources. Most people enjoy being in nature and feel good when they are interacting with the natural world. When we are in nature, we feed on its energy; it exhilarates us and recharges our strength. Making exposure to nature a regular part of your routine boosts your mood and your ability to deal with external pressures. No access to nature? Fill your living space with plants.

- **Cultivate relationships with positive people.** People can be a great source of energy, but you need to choose those who nourish you. Stay away from people who drain your power and trigger negative emotions like anger, envy, guilt, and so on. Don't let the negativity of others enter your system; don't allow anyone to trigger fear and doubt. Surround yourself with people with whom you can share your emotions, openly discuss concepts like love and gratitude, and talk about challenging milestones and the power of the Universe. Groups of people with positive outlooks on the world and on life strengthen each other. Sharing experiences makes us recognize that the Universe is consistent, discriminates against no one, and provides for everyone who reaches out for power and strength.

- **Distance yourself from negative distractions.** Don't allow negative noises into your life. Don't surrender your power to others. When negative noises do slip past your radar, don't let them scare you, weaken you, or distract you from your goals. Stay focused and be selective about what you watch, what you hear, and how you spend your time. Recognize that negative words aim to confiscate your freedom and control your behavior. Walk away from negative situations. Or, if you can look at them and recognize that they are illusions that will fall apart the moment you reject them, just avoid being pulled in. Remember that negativity only affects you if you allow it into your heart, so don't receive it; observe and don't participate in it by reacting to it.

- **Care for others after you've cared for yourself.** Helping others is a rewarding experience. But before you help others, you need to be well and strong. Allowing a burden into your life before you are strong enough will simply drain your energy. Your energy is incredibly valuable, so invest in nurturing yourself, learning, and evolving first. Then help others when you are ready!

Dream

Always make time to dream! This is one of the Universe's basic rules: Make time to visualize what you want, picture yourself achieving your dream, feel the joy of the experience, and then feel grateful for attaining it—and you will have it.

There has been a lot of scientific research around visualization, and multiple authors have argued that it leads to attainment of our dreams or goals: Jon Gabriel, author of *The Gabriel Method* (2008), shares his story about using visualization to help with his weight-loss goals. In his book *Evolve Your Brain*, Dr. Joe Dispenza (2008) talks about "mental rehearsal" and how rehearsing one's dream can produce changes in the physical body. In his book, Dr. Bruce Lipton (2016) shares his view on "the biology of belief"; he argues that our own belief limitations are the main obstacle to achieving our desired state.

Philosophers, authors, and scientists have left us clues to show us that the real power behind achieving our dreams is in our minds, our thoughts, and ourselves. Wayne Dyer, in his book *The Power of Intention*, informs us that we all have the ability to manifest and attract everything we wish to have. The list goes on.

I believe that our minds are powerful, and I believe that achieving our dreams is feasible. When I look at my own life, I can see that this has been true for me. Despite many challenging events in my life, I have always achieved my dreams. How?

Only after doing the research as an adult did I discover that I was doing exactly what the science tells us to do. I just had no idea that I was doing it—because it was natural to me, because we are designed this way, because it is one of our innate powers. For example, from the time I was a young girl, I would dream (every day!) of the man I would marry and the happy life we would share together. I would feel the happiness as if I were actually living the dream. Sure, it took years before we connected and got married—but my dream manifested itself in my reality when it was the right time.

Time seems to be a limitation for us. When we dream of something, we typically want to have it right away. But as I revealed earlier, trusting the Universe with our dreams means that we must be patient; we must trust that when it's right for us, our dreams will materialize.

Sometimes people who don't allow themselves to dream instead try to logically plan out how they will achieve their goals. They believe they are setting their own realistic expectations. But the analysis process they go through can be intimidating and can clutter their minds, leading them to think that their dream is not feasible—so they stop dreaming. But the moment you stop dreaming, you end all possibilities of the dream becoming a reality.

In truth, when people stop dreaming, what they are doing is limiting their own potential. Dreaming gives us pleasure, so there is really nothing to lose. We only feel disappointed if we have expectations. If we dream and enjoy visualizing our dreams without expectations, we can't possibly be disappointed.

Dream of feeling love—really feel it, be grateful for it—and you will find it. Dream of being healthy—really feel it, be grateful for it—and you will be guided to it. Dream of success—really imagine all aspects of it—and you will get there. Dream of something that makes you happy, something that brings you closer to inner peace. And remember, don't put a time limit on the realization part. Just enjoy the dream, work for it, and surrender it to the Universe. Never stop dreaming. You will achieve your dreams when you are ready to receive them; let the Universe decide on the timing.

▼▼▼▼▼▼▼▼▼▼▼▼▼

Try an Easy Visualization

Right now, if it's safe and comfortable to do so, sit back, close your eyes, and visualize something you've been looking forward to. Visualize the event as if it is unfolding like a movie in your mind. Begin to imagine all of the details. Use all five senses to describe what you see, feel, hear, taste, and smell. And then really experience those things, as if you are there. Add in your emotions too—allow yourself to really feel excited or thrilled or peaceful—whatever comes up for you.

Your event could be as simple as hugging your son who is studying aboard. For example, imagine you are standing in the airport waiting for him. You see the word *ARRIVED* light up on the arrivals and departures board for his flight, feel your heart pumping, watch for him to come out of the gate. And then there he is, and you're smiling, feeling the emotions of love, as you have missed him for the months he was away. Then you're hugging him, feeling the warmth of his arms around you, smelling his skin as you put your head between his neck and his shoulder . . . feeling the love, feeling the joy of having him safe next to you.

Whatever you are visualizing, dream it, feel it, and enjoy it! Dreams don't have to be complicated. They can be simple; they can be anything. As long as you can think it, you can dream it!

Sometimes we dream of achieving certain things in our life and get anxious because they don't seem to be happening fast enough or at all. Remember that you don't have a macro view of your life, and sometimes what you want now may not be what's best for you. Remember the times in your life when you didn't get something you wanted that turned out to work in your favor after all. Recall these events; they will strengthen your resolve.

Release Your Expectations

One of the most common reasons for disappointment and anxiety is the failure of our expectations.

When we are kind to someone, or we help someone, we typically do it with no motives. However, our subconscious remembers that we were kind to this person and imprints an expectation on our mind. So if this person is then unkind or ungrateful to us, our subconscious reminds us that we had been kind to this person before, and we expected that our kindness would be reciprocated. We become angry. The higher the expectations, the higher the disappointment—it's a cycle that stimulates negative emotions. Moreover, if enough of these messages dominate our subconscious, they could drive us to believe that other people don't deserve our kindness, and we may then refrain from helping or supporting others.

The reality is that when we are kind to others, we should do it for *us*, not for them. Kindness makes us feel good, and if we free our actions from expectations, we will never be disappointed—because we expect nothing in return. Our positive behaviors yield benefits to us first, before people around us choose to receive them and benefit from them. Training ourselves not to expect anything from people we help will free us from pain and disappointment.

You may be wondering, *How do I train myself to give and not expect anything in return?* Well, if you have been spending time nourishing your spiritual dimension, your needs will start to shift from ego to love. With time, the ego will no longer satisfy you; you will start seeking love for your satisfaction.

Think about it this way: If I am kind to a friend, I should enjoy my act of kindness; that is all the payback I want. Whatever my friend does becomes irrelevant because I have already harvested the results of my kindness: the joy I felt as I was being kind. If I expect anything from this friend, it will be purely to fuel my ego—this is where I never want to go!

Here are two tips on how you can do this: First, you must invest energy in doing the core step: connect, trust, and accept. It is the prerequisite for evolution. If this core step has not become a habit yet, work on it until it does. Mastering this step will equip you with the power you need to do everything else I have listed in this chapter. Second, you must allow your life to be guided by the five key principles I detailed in Chapter 9.

Here is a simple life example to help you relate. You find out that your neighbor needs a ride to work. You must decide if giving your neighbor a ride makes you happy. If yes, you do it. Your reward is feeling good. When your neighbor gets out of the car, you must close this event mentally— you release it. It's done. Any other event related to this neighbor must be viewed as a new event and not linked in any way to the ride you gave. You must picture this entire scenario before deciding if you want to give your neighbor the ride. You set your own expectation that your reward will be the pleasure you'll feel from being helpful. And that is the end. That is how you release your expectations.

The next time you are asked to do something—stay late at work, help at your child's school, attend a family function—see if you can walk yourself through the experience before agreeing. See if you can release your expectations. Do it because it satisfies you, and then close the event; let it go, not expecting anything in return.

I see the five principles— feeling gratitude, observing, nourishing my whole self, dreaming, and releasing expectations—as fundamental to how I live my life. They are core to feeling peace and having a clear vision. They have guided me and affected my attitude and outlook on life. I hand them to you and hope they will help you the way they helped me!

Chapter 10

My Parting Gift to You

No, I'm not lucky. No, I'm not special. I am nothing! But I am happy.

The same place which I originally blamed for my hardship—Lebanon—is now my heaven. So, you see, it was never about "this place"; it's about how I receive life! I'm happy because I figured out how to tap into the power made available to me—to all of us. This power is here for every one of us, and it multiplies when more people connect to it. When you reach out to nourish your energy from this power source, you are making the power contagious—you essentially affect everyone around you. This is what we want: to share this power so that more people can tap into the energy. So test it, tap into it, and discover its value. You have nothing to lose!

Life doesn't need to be difficult. We can choose to hate or to understand. We can choose to receive the cruelty of others or reject it. We can choose to suppress others or to trigger their passions. We can choose to forgive or let our anger destroy us. Most importantly, we can choose to use the universal power available to us or to disconnect from it and weaken ourselves. It's all up to us—we make the choice.

Even if we do take the wrong turn at times, remember that the moment we connect, we will see clearly again and we can adjust our path. We are never permanently lost; we are just delayed.

I hope this book has inspired you to calm your mind, because only then will you be ready to enjoy your journey and start asking questions. Only with a calm mind will you be able to see beyond the clutter, and only then can you see the answers when they materialize in front of you.

My first wish for you is to practice the core step every day: take the time to connect, trust, and accept the universal power available to you. My second wish is for you to practice the five principles: Make room for gratitude, be an observer, nourish your whole self, never stop dreaming, and let go of expectations. With time, they will become second nature and infuse your character. And my third wish is that you evolve your spirituality and achieve your personal dreams.

As you apply the notions presented in this book to your day-to-day life, I hope you will track how much stronger you become, how more at peace you feel, and how more elevated the emotions you experience are. The pleasure of being in an evolved state will drive your commitment to stay there. Because, trust me, you won't want to feel anything but positive feelings.

Resources

We are lucky that we live in this era. Resources are available to us if we choose to learn and connect. Here are some resources that either triggered elevated emotions for me, made me think, validated what I already knew and felt, or made me feel part of a bigger community of truth seekers.

You are the master of what you allow into your mind! These writings added some value to my thinking and to my life. I hope that they can widen the scope of your thinking as well.

Books

Action Learning in Action: Transforming Problems and People for World-Class Organizational Learning, by Michael J. Marquardt

The Biology of Belief: Unleashing the Power of Consciousness, Matter, and Miracles, by Bruce H. Lipton

Breaking the Habit of Being Yourself: How to Lose Your Mind and Create a New One, by Dr. Joe Dispenza

Devices for Monitoring Nonphysical Energies, by William A. Tiller

The Divine Matrix: Bridging Time, Space, Miracles, and Belief, by Gregg Braden

Evolve Your Brain: The Science of Changing Your Mind, by Dr. Joe Dispenza

The God Code: The Secret of Our Past, the Promise of Our Future, by Gregg Braden

The Nature of Human Values, by Milton Rokeach

Pineal Gland & Your Third Eye: Proven Methods to Develop Your Higher Self, by Jill Ammon-Wexler

Science and Human Transformation: Subtle Energies, Intentionality, and Consciousness, by William A. Tiller

Selling Spirituality: The Silent Takeover of Religion, by Jeremy Carrette and Richard King

Spiritual Solutions: Answers to Life's Greatest Challenges, by Deepak Chopra

Toward a Psychology of Being, by Abraham H. Maslow

The Wisdom of Your Cells: How Your Beliefs Control Your Biology, by Bruce H. Lipton

Scholarly Articles

Alderfer, C. P. (1969). "An Empirical Test of a New Theory of Human Needs." *Organizational Behavior and Human Performance* 4(2): 142–175.

Gerhart, B., and Fang, M. (2005). "National Culture and Human Resource Management: Assumptions and Evidence." *International Journal of Human Resource Management* 16(6): 971–986.

Lips-Wiersma, M., and Mills, A. J. (2014). "Understanding the Basic Assumptions About Human Nature in Workplace Spirituality Beyond the Critical Versus Positive Divide." *Journal of Management Inquiry* 23(2): 148–161.

Marshall, J. (1999). "Living Life as Inquiry." *Systemic Practice and Action* 12(2): 155–171.

Marshall, J., and Reason, P. (2007). "Quality in Research as 'Taking an Attitude of Inquiry.'" *Management Research News* 30(5): 368–380.

Stephen T., et al. (2011). "Maslow's Hierarchy of Human Needs and the Adoption of Health-Related Technologies for Older Adults." *Ageing International* 37(4): 1–19.

Naidoo, M. (2014). "The Potential of Spiritual Leadership in Workplace Spirituality." *Koers – Bulletin for Christian Scholarship* 79(2): 01–08.

Sheep, M. L. (2006). "Nurturing the Whole Person: The Ethics of Workplace Spirituality in a Society of Organizations." *Journal of Business Ethics* 66: 357–375.

Smith, E. (2011). "Teaching Critical Reflection." *Teaching in Higher Education* 16(2): 211–223.

Thielke, S., et al. (2011). "Maslow's Hierarchy of Human Needs and the Adoption of Health-Related Technologies for Older Adults." *Ageing International* 37(4): 1–19.

References

Baker, S. (2009). "Fear, Get Out of My Life Forever." Collierville, TN: Instantpublisher.com.

Braden, G. (2008). *The Divine Matrix: Bridging Time, Space, Miracles, and Belief.* Carlsbad, CA: Hay House.

Bou-Diab, N. K. (2020). *Spirituality in the Organization.* University of Liverpool.

Chopra, D. (2012). *Spiritual Solutions: Answers to Life's Greatest Challenges.* New York: Harmony Books.

Dispenza, J. (2008). *Evolve Your Brain: The Science of Changing Your Mind.* Health Communications.

Dispenza, J. (2012). *Breaking the Habit of Being Yourself: How to Lose Your Mind and Create a New One.* Carlsbad, CA: Hay House.

Dyer, W. (2015). *The Power of Intention.* Carlsbad, CA: Hay House.

Ellerby, J. H. (2015). *Inspiration Deficit Disorder.* London: Hay House.

Fehr, E., and Hoff, K. (2011). "Introduction: Tastes, Castes and Culture: The Influence of Society on Preferences." *The*

Economic Journal 131 (556): F396–F412.

Gabriel, J. (2008). *The Gabriel Method: The Revolutionary Diet-Free Way to Totally Transform Your Body.* New York: Atria Books.

Gomes, O. (2011). "The Hierarchy of Human Needs and Their Social Valuation." *International Journal of Social Economics* 38 (3): 237–259.

HeartMath Institute. https://www.heartmath.org/research/

Kolb, D. A. (1983). *Experiential Learning as the Science of Learning and Development.* Upper Saddle River, NJ: Prentice Hall.

László, E. (2017). *The Intelligence of the Cosmos: Why Are We Here? New Answers from the Frontiers of Science.* Rochester, VT: Inner Traditions.

Lipton, B. H. (2016). *The Biology of Belief: Unleashing the Power of Consciousness, Matter, and Miracles.* London: Hay House.

Marquardt, M. J. (1999). *Action Learning in Action: Transforming Problems and People for World-Class Organizational Learning.* Palo Alto, CA: Davies-Black.

Marshall, J. (1999). "Living Life as Inquiry." *Systemic Practice and Action Research*, 12 (2): 155–171.

McCraty, R., Atkinson, M., and Bradley, R. (2004). "Electrophysiological Evidence of Intuition: Part 1. The Surprising Role of the Heart." *The Journal of Alternative and Complementary Medicine* 10 (1): 133–14.

www.ingramcontent.com/pod-product-compliance
Lightning Source LLC
Chambersburg PA
CBHW071240070526
44583CB00017B/2267